I0798997

Praise for The Murder of Sheriff W.W. Withers and Other Historic Eugene Cases

It is easy to look at a photograph from one hundred years ago and think, "things were a lot simpler then," and assume that people's lives were too. However, when we dig below the surface, read the letters and explore the records they left behind, it becomes clear how sophisticated, industrious, passionate and sometimes destructive their lives actually were. The Murder of Sheriff W.W. Withers *explores some of Lane County's most interesting crime stories and gives us amazing insight into the people involved.*

—Robin Myers, Lane County History Museum

Here's proof that pioneer Eugene, Oregon, was part of the Wild West: six-gun murders, grisly deaths and public hangings, all carefully researched by articulate local historian Jen Chambers.

—William L. Sullivan, author of Exploring Oregon's History

THE MURDER OF SHERIFF W.W. WITHERS
AND OTHER HISTORIC EUGENE CASES

JENNIFER CHAMBERS

THE History PRESS

Published by The History Press
An imprint of Arcadia Publishing
Charleston, SC
www.historypress.com

First published 2025

Manufactured in the United States

ISBN 9781467158800

Library of Congress Control Number: 2025934733

CONTENTS

ACKNOWLEDGEMENTS

I had finished a talk at the Lane County Historic Museum about my last book, *Murder & Mayhem in the Willamette Valley*, when the museum curator, Robin, came to me with an incredible story and the opportunity of a lifetime. The curator had been cataloging each item after the museum was closed for a huge remodel. In one of the first boxes, she found a photo portrait of a man with kind eyes and an incredible mustache. She put him on the mantel of the museum's main room and talked to him companionably over the next months as the museum was reimagined and the exhibits were replaced piece by piece. Others were creeped out that his eyes seemed to follow you across the room, but Robin chatted with him as she helped reorganize and thought of him as a good guy.

In the second-to-last box, she found the name card that went with the portrait. She now knew the name of Sheriff W.W. Withers, one of Eugene's most beloved sheriffs, and she was able to place it next to his portrait. In the last box, she found a small white fabric bag. Tipping the contents out into her hand, she found a tied rope noose, severed at the end as if it had been cut from the scaffold. The tag with it said it belonged to the man who killed the esteemed sheriff, Eliott Lyons. She was dying to find out the whole story and hoped I might want to find out more. I was dying to find out too. Later, Robin found a previously uncatalogued box crammed with the records of the Eugene coroner from 1865 to 1913. She allowed me to read this treasure trove of undiscovered stories of Eugene's past. Many of their stories are in this book.

This book is due to the hard work of Robin Myers and the fabulous Lane County History Museum. Any good researcher and author can appreciate the value of a good museum. This book wouldn't exist without the museum. A huge help came from Russ Carey, who compiled an incredible amount of information in his unpublished manuscript "The Murder of Sheriff William Washington Withers." It was a boon to be able to confirm, deny or figure out things I needed to know with the help of your work. Thanks go also to Jan and Mike from the Find a Grave website and all their hard work.

Joel Petersdorf generously shared his family lore, information and photographs. I could not have had such a full picture of the events surrounding the double tragedy without his help, his pictures or his directions—I owe him a lot and am very grateful. One of my most interesting moments writing this book was when Joel provided the location of his family's homestead, and Robin found the plat and county records, so I could play history detective and physically try to go there. It's remote still, fertile, and beautiful.

As always, this book is dedicated to my family, who put up with my writing schedule and the way I drag us to every historical wayside, museum and monument. It's also dedicated to my grandma Patricia A. Byers, who died at 99½ during the writing of this book. My "Grammy" was our family's historian. She spent countless hours researching the story of our ancestors at a time when it meant sifting through microfiche and cold-calling possible relations. Through her stories, I went back to the early 1700s, when my eight-times-great grandfather let General George Washington's army sleep in his field, and the 1860s, when a later relative was a conductor on the Underground Railroad and way, way back to when our people were simple (very poor) cattlemen in Ireland. Those stories made me fascinated to learn about the real-life stories of people from history. Grammy told me she wouldn't make it to 100 the last time she was sick, but she had always rallied, and I laughed it away as an older version of "39 and holding." Maybe she had a touch more "knowing" than I gave her credit for. I told her all about this book the last time I saw her.

1

THE MURDER OF SHERIFF W.W. WITHERS AND THE LAST HANGING IN LANE COUNTY

W.W. (William Washington) Withers was, by all accounts, a good and honorable man, which made the way he died even more tragic. It all started with some horse thieves, Withers's determined pursuit of justice and career criminal Eliott Lyons's desperate flight for freedom that turned to murder.

W.W. Withers was both well-known and well-loved in his community. He was born near Corvallis, Oregon, on January 1, 1860. His parents moved the large family from Looking Glass Valley in Douglas County to a farm about two and a half miles outside Eugene when he was about ten years old. After growing up and going through the local school system, Withers married and moved to his own farm in Fall Creek, fourteen and a half miles outside Eugene. He lived there with his wife and one son, Frank, when he was first nominated for sheriff of Lane County, and he won the election by the barest margin of only 25 votes. His regard locally can be measured by how much his votership increased the next go-around. The second time he was nominated, in 1902, he had moved to Eugene proper and won the election by 794 votes.[1]

Withers was reported as being a diligent sheriff with an impressive arrest record and generally upholding the law at all times. In 1900, he rather heroically helped capture runaway criminal Pete McDonald, who stole "between 30 and 40 gold watches, 65 gold rings and a considerable quantity of other jewelry," from a jewelry store in Junction City, Oregon.

Above: Lane County Sheriff W.W. Withers seated in his office, circa 1895. *Lane County History Museum.*

Opposite: The J.E.P. Withers family photo, undated. *In front, left to right*: Emma (Cornelius), J.E.P. Withers (father), Jessie (Edmiston), Margaret Sloan Gillespie Withers (mother) and Anna (Emery). *In back, left to right*: Allie (Hawley), Price Withers, Mabel (Bogart), W.W. Withers and Mary (Van Duyn). *Lane County History Museum.*

In conjunction with detectives in Salem, Withers determined that McDonald had fled there and tried to fence the stolen goods in that city, when a woman reported that she had been approached on the street:

> *In the course of her questioning, the stranger produced a small Bible, the back of which she casually discovered the name Pete McDonald, Tacoma. As soon as the authorities got this clew* [sic] *the officers felt that pursuit of McDonald was the surest way to catch the burglar.*[2]

As if in a script from an old movie, McDonald didn't make a very good burglar, even though he had escaped notice in the past. After some questioning around town, the detectives found that he had

rented a room for the night at a local hotel, and the chambermaid found a large quantity of gold jewelry and watches in the space between the mattress and the wall. The officers found out too late and were told he had run to the Sound in Washington. Sheriff Withers was going through that area, caught him there and returned to Lane County with both burglar and his loot in tow. The city praised Withers for his persistence, and the paper reported that "McDonald is well known in that section as a bad case, but so completely did he disappear after his burglary that had it not been for the accidental tracing, he might have disposed of the plunder without being discovered."

Sheriff Withers was conscientious. Many issues of newspapers all over Lane County mentioned his presence in their cities in the "Personal" or "About Town" sections, evidence that he crisscrossed the valley in his role. In December 1898, he even escorted a Miss Fannie Winter on a visit to her sister in the Insane Asylum in Salem. Mrs. Laura Hanks, twenty-five, was suffering from what was then called "insanity caused by brain fever," and Sheriff Withers acted as Miss Winter's guard and brought her safely to and from Eugene.[3] The good sheriff had to travel far and wide to complete his duties, which ranged from solving bank robbery to small-time theft, property crime and a myriad of other tasks. In August 1901, Withers himself rode north of Eugene to Corvallis to return a horse that had been stolen in July rather than send a deputy; he had caught the culprit when he tried to sell the animal using an alias.[4]

In his run for reelection in 1900, Sheriff Withers's campaign ads made much of his superiority to his predecessor, Sheriff Jones, noting that during Jones's four years in power he "took 12 criminals to the state penitentiary," while Sheriff Withers' record was "in 12 months Withers took 16 and executed 1."[5]

The sheriff's personally written news bulletins and wanted posters let his personality shine through. One of the most evocative bulletins reads:

Eugene—Sheriff W.W. Withers rounded up a gang of 11 hobos in the woods beyond the river opposite Eugene and took them to the city jail. Residents beyond the river had complained that many of their chickens were missing. At the camp of the hobos preparations for a big chicken dinner were going on.[6]

The "Wanted" signs he wrote were similarly human-sounding in tone. They denote a particular eye for detail and sound ferocious and dogged in his chase. This reward poster for the arrest of Henry Day, who is featured elsewhere in this book, is a great example of his language:

$100 Reward
Arrest for Embezzlement
Description: Henry J. Day, age about 40 years; height about 6 feet; weighs 210 pounds; dark hair not very long; generally combs pompadour; dark mustache; dark blue eyes; fair complexion; pleasing personality and makes friends easily; wore dark suit of clothes and dark overcoat with felt collar.... In walking, sets heels down hard and raises on toes; drops shoulders with each step; smokes cigarettes habitually and blows smoke upward through mustache; constantly hawks and spits.

The last sentence is the most telling of the man who wrote it:

I hold warrant and want to arrest this man bad. Arrest and hold him and wire me.[7]

Sheriff W.W. Withers was a good sheriff, one who cared passionately about the people he was sworn to protect. One paper even said:

It can be truthfully said that he was the most popular sherriff [sic] *that Lane County ever had. He was fearless in his duties as an officer, and bore the reputation of catching every criminal he went after.*[8]

Though he was a Lane County sheriff, Withers traveled widely for his job. The *Eugene Weekly Guard* acted as one of his most vocal supporters, which is almost amusing today, when press are as inclined to vitriol as to praise:

Sheriff Withers is a very busy man these days. He is kept constantly on the jump. The latter part of last week he was up in the Fall Creek country.

> *Tuesday noon of this week he arrived home from the Gate Creek country on the upper McKenzie....These trips were all made for the purpose of serving subpoenas and other papers. Monday, after returning from Blue River, the sheriff will start for Florence....Mr. Withers makes all these trips throughout the county on the hurricane deck* [the roof or upper deck] *of a cayuse* [boat].[9]

As much as he was loved, he naturally had enemies. One of those was recidivist criminal thirty-five-year-old Eliott Lyons. Lyons, a known horse thief, had been on the run for the theft of some horses in eastern Oregon. Eliott had evaded capture for the theft of horses in Josephine County and found himself out of options. He was forced to return to hole up on his parents' homestead outside Eugene, on Wildcat Creek near the town of Walton. The sheriff knew Lyons's relatives lived in his jurisdiction and kept watch for the thief. When Sheriff Withers was notified, he and Deputy Jack Smith rode up to neighbor William Cornelius's farm and deputized him in their haste to catch Lyons.

A photo of Lyons's relatives was alluded to in the *Eugene Guard* on October 25, 1902, with this paragraph. There was no mention if the "well-known" reference to the Lyons clan was for being infamous, or popular, or pious:

> *The Guard today was shown a group picture of W.F. Lyons and family of twelve children. It is a very good picture of that well-known Lane County family. It consists of the father and mother and the following twelve children: Mrs. Sallie Davis, Charles Lyons, Ben Lyons, Mrs. Hettie Renshaw, Mrs. Nancy Goodpasture, Vint Lyons, Eliott Lyons, Mrs. Rose Hill, Mrs. Belle Rowland, Mrs. May Everett, Tracy Lyons and Scott Lyons.*[10]

William Cornelius's son Roy was about seven or eight years old at the time his father was deputized. He was interviewed by Hallie Hills Huntington as part of the Oregon Historical Society Oral History interviews in 1976 and recounted the story his father told him after his return from the Lyons homestead.

> *They took the three of them, rode down and this house where Eliott was staying with his folks was up kinda on the hillside and there was a kind of brushy road all around, lots of brush around the house, and they tied the horses below the road and walked up. Well, the house had a kitchen door and one off the dining room and one off the living room, and the lower part of the house was up six or seven steps to get up on the porch.*

The diagram and understanding of the house architecture is an important point and would figure prominently in the coroner's report of the incident to follow. Cornelius continued:

> *And my father was deputized to take the porch on the south and Sheriff Withers was supposed to go around to the front door. Well, just as my father stepped up on the porch he could see Eliott Lyons in there reading a newspaper and he had his six-shooter laying on the table right next to him, and just about that time Mrs. Lyons, his mother, opened the kitchen door to throw the dish water out, and Sheriff Smith* [sic] *or Deputy Smith, said, "Shut the door madam, the house is surrounded."*

The official coroner's report differs on this next part of the story. Cornelius said that this was how events transpired:

> *At that, Eliott Lyons jumped up and grabbed his gun. She* [his wife, Elizabeth Lyons] *ran out with him into the living room and just about the time Sheriff Withers came in and Mr. Lyons* [Eliott's father] *grabbed him by the arm and run right past the Sheriff and as he went past him he shot him in the neck and he fell.*

In William Cornelius's official statement to the coroner, he concurred and stated:

> *Q (Coroner)—What was the next thing you heard?*
> *A—The next thing I heard was Mr. Withers saying, "Let go; let me loose; let loose I tell you," about 4 times.*
> *Q—How loud was his voice at the time?*
> *A—A little louder than usual.*
> *Q—Anyone else speak?*
> *A—No, Sir.*
> *Q—You heard him say, "Let go; let me loose; let loose I tell you," about 4 times?*
> *A—Yes, Sir.*
> *Q—Where did it sound like he was?*
> *A—It sounded like he was about along in here* [pointing, about middle of sitting room].
> *Q—How long after you heard Mr. Withers speak was it before you heard the pistol shot?*
> *A—Just that quick* [showing with thumb and finger].

Cornelius saw two women as he burst into the room, one inside the room and one going into the bedroom, which was at the rear of the sitting room. Deputy Smith, who had burst in a moment before Cornelius, was on Withers's right side as he lay on the floor with his head to the west. Cornelious estimated six minutes after the shooting before they picked him up and placed him on the lounge, or long couch. The coroner went on to ask about Withers's state when he was found.

Q—What was the first words that Mr. Withers spoke to you and Mr. Smith?
A—When we got to him he said, "Boys he shot me and run out over me and went out through that door and he is gone."
Q—Did he say anything about what the women and his father had done?
A—He says, "I could have got him all right but he had a hold of me but I could have shot him but I didn't want to kill him." He told us that several times.

After some questions verifying the lights, carpet and furnishings, the coroner circled back.

Q—Did Billy, Mr. Withers, make any statement in regard to how the shooting was done?
A—He said, "Boys. I want to tell you how it was done; I might be done up; they all had hold of me and I kept telling them to let loose of me and they held me until he shot me and run and then they let go."
Q—Just repeat the statement Mr. Withers made.
A—He said, "They was holding me and I told them to let go and they wouldn't do it and Eliott shot me and run out over me and out through the front door," and Vint was with me at the time, not Charley....He said, "Boys, I want to tell you how it was done, for I want you to see that they are pulled." I was there and we were rubbing his hands.

He ended his questioning with:

Q—Did Mr. Withers state to you that this man had said he would not be taken alive or about any threats Eliott had made?
A—No, sir.

Tracy Lyons, twenty-two, Eliott's younger brother, was next to be questioned. The coroner went through a line of questioning regarding whether Eliott had been heard saying something about what he would do if he were to be caught.

Q—Is it not a fact, Tracy, that Eliott told you what he would do if an officer tried to arrest him?
A—No, sir. I heard him say, "they don't want to bother me," and that was the only words I ever heard him say. Something to that effect.
Q—Did you see Mr. Withers last Thursday?
A—Yes.
Q—Where were you at the time you saw him?
A—About a mile and a half this side of our place.
Q—What, if anything, did he say to you?
A—Well, he asked if he (Eliott) was there, and I told him he was, and he said, "Boys, I can't let you go on; you must go back and wait."

The coroner wanted to clarify this response.

Q—What did you do then?
A—Well, they left there, this Mr. Smith and Cornelius—the house is about 100 yards of the road and we ran up to the house, and Mr. Smith and Mr. Cornelius came by there on their way to where Mr. Withers as waiting for them and Mr. Smith and Billy Cornelius called Walter Chastain down there to talk to him, I supposed, and after Mr. Chastain came back to the house. I just made the remark to him. I said, "Walter, I'm afraid someone will get hurt down there to-night," and he said, "Why do you think so, Tracy?" and I said, "Because, Walter, they will go into the house and surprise him and won't wait. I'm afraid something will happen if they do that." That was all I told him.

Tracy goes on to tell the coroner how scared he was that his brother wouldn't think first if confronted and that Eliott might hurt the policemen. He also relayed that he saw that Eliott had a Smith & Wesson .32-caliber revolver in his possession. Although Tracy was contrite in hindsight, he was most sorry that he might have been able to warn the sheriff and saved his life.

Q—Did he, your brother Eliott, ever come back to the house after the shot was fired?
A—No, sir. I can say that.

Q—Did he ever say to you that he would shoot any man that would attempt to arrest him?
A—I think he did say something like that.

Later on in the interview, Tracy revealed an important point:

Q (by Mr. Williams)—You may state, Tracy, just what Eliott told you, in his own language.
A—Well, as near as I can tell. It has been nearly two months ago, that we were grubbing down [digging for food] *in the meadow, he and me, and he said to me, "Tracy, what would you do if you were in my place if the sheriff would come after you?" I said, "Eliott, I would just drop everything and go and stand a trial." Then he studied* [sic] *a little while and said, "I wouldn't. I don't want them to bother around me." Just as good as to say he would kill the first man that tried to arrest him.*

Charles Lyons, forty-eight, another brother of Eliott's, provided his experience of that day. His home was near his father's house, about four hundred yards due west. He had been standing on his porch, looking for the younger boys to come home, and encountered his nephew Ernest, who told him that Eliott had "shot somebody." Charles Lyons ran "every step of the way" to his father's house. When he arrived, he found Sheriff Withers, shot but not yet dead. Withers was lying on his back.

Q (by Coroner)—Now, Mr. Lyons, did he [the sheriff] *say anything to you when he you first approached him?*
A—Well, when he told me that "He had done me up," I said, "I reckon not Will," and he says, "When he shot me I just dropped; I couldn't move," and that's the way I found him when I got there."

Charles Lyons; another brother, Vint Lyons; Deputy Smith; and William Cornelius carried Withers to the lounge. Immediately, Withers requested that they bring him to a doctor in town. Charles retrieved his wagon for the trip. As he did so, the smaller boys and Vint warmed large rocks in the coals to make Withers comfortable on the drive.

Q—Did he say anything else?
A—Well, not right at that time. I left then and I went home and got my team and when I got back Scott was there, my other brother, and him and

Vint, one on each side of him, were working with him and rubbing his hands and I heard him say, "I don't blame any of you folks, I went at this wrong," or "I did wrong." I don't just remember positively what he said.

The coroner ascertained Sheriff Withers's state of mind as being rational with several questions. Then he asked Lyons what Eliott's wife said had happened.

A—Well, she said that she never—that is, when the kitchen door was opened first, Will and Eliott met right there and she saw who was there and she called Eliott and was standing by the side of him and had a hold of him when he shot Will. That was where she was.
Q (Jury)—Who did she say she had a hold of?
A—Eliott; her husband.

Deputy J.S. Stiles, when interviewed, testified to the statement he had been given by Lyons Senior.

A—I first asked Mr. Lyons if he knew who Withers was when he first came in the house. He told me that he did. I asked him if he had an idea what the errand was. He told me that he did. I asked him if the family were near when Mr. Withers entered the house. He told me they were sitting around the fireplace. I have the diagram here. He said that when Mr. Withers came in, he called to his son Eliott to stop and that he caught his son in the door between the sitting room and the dining room. This being the door right here [pointing to diagram], *and he, Mr. Withers took his son by the coat collar with his left hand. He pushed him back through the door with his back against the fireplace. He said that he could see Withers with a revolver in his right hand holding it up somewhere near a level with his son's face, and about that time he heard a shot and Withers fell. I asked him if any of the family interfered in any way. He told me no. I then says, "Is it not a fact that some one of the family got Mr. Withers' arm and pulled it down?" He answered no again. I asked him where Mrs. Eliott Lyons was when Smith came in. He told me she was in this bedroom here. That about ends his statement as far as I can tell.*

Stiles was asked about statements given by Elizabeth Lyons, Eliott's wife. She cried when asked about where Withers had fallen, and he reported that it was not a useful interview.

The coroner called Elizabeth Lyons, thirty-seven, to the stand. She stated that she had heard a whistle and thought that it was the younger boys coming home, so she opened the door. Someone told her gruffly to go back into the house, as it was surrounded. She stated that Withers had a hold of her husband's arm. Elizabeth Lyons went up to the sheriff, laid her hand on his shoulder and said, "For God's sake, don't do this." She further stated that the elder Mrs. Lyons had a hold of the sheriff's arm as well, though she "couldn't be positive." The older Mr. Lyons was present in the room, and both had a hold of Withers's non-shooting arm.

The next interview was with the attending doctor, Dr. D.A. Payne, forty-nine. He testified that the sheriff was "suffering from a gunshot wound to the neck, inflicting a wound in immediate line below the larynx." The .32- or .38-caliber bullet went through the trachea, esophagus and seventh cervical vertebra and stopped at the base of the skull. The coroner asked if the doctor had been able to speak to the sheriff while the injured man was still alive.

> *A—At about 4:30 o'clock on Friday afternoon, I had a conversation with Mr. Withers. I told him that I supposed he understood the grave nature of the injury and that he was likely not recover and he said that he wanted to talk to me something about the injury and I asked him if he was shot by Mr. Lyons and he said that at the time of the shooting, he had him under arrest. I asked if Lyons' wife or mother or father interfered and took hold of him and he said they took hold of him when he had him arrested. I said to him, "Then they interfered and took hold of you?" and he said, "yes, that's right."*

Dr. Payne said that Withers nodded his head and spoke loudly to be heard across the room. He wanted to talk to his wife and repeated his story that the family had held him back several times. The bullet, which penetrated the spinal cord, paralyzed the sheriff from the neck down and would have been fatal in any event. He was clear-minded when he first spoke to the doctor and became semiconscious about thirty minutes after the doctor's arrival.

Eliott Lyons escaped as he ran through the cabin door, and no sign of him was found until three days later. His wife, Mrs. Lyons, was arrested and charged with being an accessory to a felony. After the conclusion of his trial, authorities expected to try her for the same.

After Lyons's arrest, it was found that when he ran off from the scene of the crime, he hid overnight and "slept in a pile of railroad ties near Goshen," on the other side of Eugene. Before that, he'd passed through Eugene and

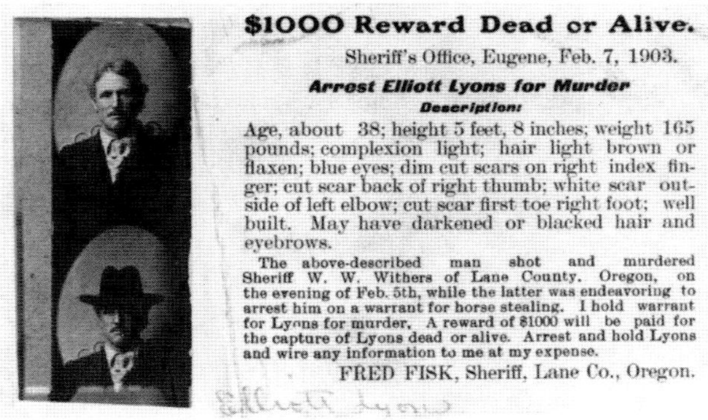
$1000 Reward Dead or Alive.

Sheriff's Office, Eugene, Feb. 7, 1903.

Arrest Elliott Lyons for Murder

Description:

Age, about 38; height 5 feet, 8 inches; weight 165 pounds; complexion light; hair light brown or flaxen; blue eyes; dim cut scars on right index finger; cut scar back of right thumb; white scar outside of left elbow; cut scar first toe right foot; well built. May have darkened or blacked hair and eyebrows.

The above-described man shot and murdered Sheriff W. W. Withers of Lane County, Oregon, on the evening of Feb. 5th, while the latter was endeavoring to arrest him on a warrant for horse stealing. I hold warrant for Lyons for murder. A reward of $1000 will be paid for the capture of Lyons dead or alive. Arrest and hold Lyons and wire any information to me at my expense.

FRED FISK, Sheriff, Lane Co., Oregon.

Advertisement offering $1,000 reward "Dead or Alive" for the arrest of Eliott Lyons, who murdered Lane County Sheriff W.W. Withers on February 5, 1903, when Withers was trying to arrest him for stealing horses. Detailed description of Lyons's appearance includes two photos. Ad is signed by Lane County Sheriff Fred Fisk. *Lane County History Museum.*

went to the home of Dr. Atwood, whose horses he occasionally took care of, and changed his clothes there to disguise himself as a "tramp."

He was caught at eight o'clock in the morning trying to jump on board a freight train in Creswell. When he was arrested, he was unarmed and said he couldn't remember where he dropped his gun. He thought it might be in the creek near his parents' home or in the Willamette River. When caught, he had been in Creswell for almost sixty minutes and was "about exhausted from his flight across the country in stormy weather."[11]

His jail stay was punctuated by intrigue, as mobs intermittently threatened to lynch Lyons. When interviewed in jail, he complained that his leg hurt him and stated that he would not have given himself up voluntarily. Additionally, he said that he would have shot anyone who tried to take him in. During his jail stay, a reporter asked Lyons where he had put the gun. He said,

> *I do not remember what became of the thing. I decided it was all up when I crossed the Long Tom and was so wet and tired. I did not care what happened to me then. It was out there by Cook's place I lost my pistol and I did not care enough about anything to look for it. I have been unarmed for three days.*[12]

The reporter asked more about where Lyons was during his flight from justice. Eliott Lyons gave an accounting of the places he had hidden: the horse yard, a straw stack, breakfast with an unaware family of German descent and then the train yard. Then the reporter asked him why he killed the sheriff:

> *Oh, I told him I wouldn't go with him, and wanted to be stubborn, I guess. My wife commenced to plead for me, and I saw a small chance to get away.*

> *Billie didn't have his gun pulled, so I thought I would hold him up and force him to let go. He held me by the coat, and I had my gun in my pocket. I just pointed it at him from my side when I saw the chance and fired. I wished I hadn't right away, but I ran as fast as I could.*[13]

The *Bohemia Nugget* gave a veritable sermon on evil living in its article on his sentencing, although the author gave a good background:

> *From boyhood, shiftless and worthless; a drawback to his family, a disgrace to the woman who was foolish enough to marry him. A man who, according to reports, would rather steal then earn an honest living. Always planning how to secure a meal and a bed without physical exertion. As the years came and went, his misdemeanors increased and took on the form of actual crime.*

The sermon got more florid as it went through the criminal's life:

> *His release from prison walls, instead of prompting him to do better, had the effect to make him still more lawless, thieving and reckless. At last he became a fugitive from justice. Then the vengeful spirit of the brutal, cowardly thief took possession of him and he determined to have his liberty no matter what the cost.*[14]

The trial was not a long one. It began on the morning of March 3 and was over before dark. The most sensational part of the trial came at four o'clock in the afternoon, when a group of women brought Eliott Lyon's mother in on a litter of pillows. Her testimony contradicted the previous version of events. Her story was that on the day the murder was committed, she never heard Sheriff Withers speak but instead herself begged to know why her son was being arrested. Her husband, Lyons Senior, said the same thing.[15] Neither was ever charged with accessory to murder for holding back Sheriff Withers.

The jury was not out for long when they went into deliberation. A scant ten minutes after they cloistered themselves, the verdict was in: guilty of murder in the first degree. As was custom, invitations to view the hanging were sent to people pertinent to the case. It was held in public, behind the Lane County Courthouse. Ray Cornelius, son of the deputized-for-the-occasion William Cornelius, gave his account of what his father said happened on April 17, 1903:

So, they built about an eight-foot board fence around the jail in Eugene, and it was where the courthouse, just west of the courthouse, on the block west of the courthouse, and they put up thirteen steps, put their platform up, and my father went down to watch the hanging. He said they led Eliot up the steps, walked out on the trap door. They asked if he had anything to say. He said, "No."

They put a black hood down over his head, put the hang knot at the bottom of his ear, drew it up tight and there were three ropes running from the trap door up to where there were three people with their big butcher knives, and as they gave the signal they all cut the ropes. No one knows which one was attached to the door but my father said that, uh, his neck stretched out towards two feet long, and that he would never want to see another hanging. He'd never see one as long as he lived.[16]

Eliott Lyons's death was described thus in the *Eugene Weekly Guard*:

Edward Eliott Lyon this morning at 9:31 o'clock dropped to his death through the scaffold floor in expiation of his crime.

The man whose thread of life was cut today in accordance of the conviction by jury and sentence of the court, is Edward Eliott Lyons, of Walton, Lane County. He is of medium stature, wearer of a cynical but forlorn expression; confessed slayer of the brave sheriff, on the 5th day of last February, while the official was in the act of doing his duty as officer of the law.[17]

Lyons's death would be the last official hanging to occur in Lane County as a consequence of being found guilty of crimes. In 1903, the legislature of the State of Oregon placed an amendment on state law. All executions were brought out of public view and held in the Oregon State Penitentiary. Capital punishment was abolished in the state in 1914, reinstated in 1920, repealed in 1964, reinstated in 1978 and made unconstitutional by the Oregon Supreme Court in 1981. However, the voters put the punishment back in 1984, flouting the supreme court ruling. In 2011, Governor John Kitzhaber stopped the practice by the declaration of a moratorium, citing his personal conviction that he "not be a part of the compromised and inequitable system." The Oregon Supreme Court agreed and allowed the moratorium to stand as long as he was in office. The next governor, Kate Brown, continued the practice pending a consensus on how to make the system fair. She commuted the seventeen sentences on Oregon's Death Row in 2022. Those sentences have been changed to life without parole, and as of this writing, they remain the same.[18]

Eliott Lyons was buried in an unmarked pauper's grave in the Oregon Pioneer Cemetery.[19]

The new sheriff of Eugene, Sheriff Storey, visited Lyons before his death. He described Lyons with a very pointed insight:

> *All I can say is that he does not look like a criminal, but instead more like an idiot. His cheekbones are high, and his chin comes to a point; there does not seem to be the firmness about him that you usually find in a criminal. He does not seem capable of weighing things as keenly as many men you would meet.*

Storey made some strong remarks to Lyons about the mess he was in and how much trouble he had caused. The new sheriff then asked him why he did it. "And he replied," the sheriff said, "that he did not know himself."[20]

There is no record of Lyons's parents being served with any kind of consequence for allegedly holding back Sheriff Withers so that their son could at best escape or, at worst, harm the sheriff. Many references in court documents, newspaper articles and the coroner's report spoke of their agedness and ill health. Elizabeth Lyons was to have been arraigned immediately after her husband, but what happened to her after her husband's death has yet to be uncovered. The matter may have been dropped after her husband was sentenced to die.

A notice of a marriage appeared in local papers in November 1906 between "Chas. (Charles) E. & Lizzie E. Lyons," as well as a sale of eighty acres of land from the couple to one T.J. Davis and eighty acres to a person named S.H. Lyons. It is possible, then, to surmise that Mrs. Elizabeth (Eliott) Lyons later became Mrs. Elizabeth (Charles) Lyons, although there is no definitive find proof of that.[21]

2

"MORE THAN I CAN STAND!"

The Deaths of Sanford and Emma Skinner

Sanford Skinner was a prosperous farmer when he and his wife, Emma, were killed on June 1, 1905, in the Mohawk Valley east of Eugene. The couple, who were "well-to-do and one of the best families in Lane County," were killed by a man they had taken in as a boarder, Emma's brother, John Richards, at 5:30 a.m. on the morning of June 1, 1905.

Sanford Skinner was born on March 2, 1839, in Lane County, Oregon. His father, Marion Harper Skinner, was a former Civil War soldier from Iowa, and later Nebraska, before he became the postmaster after moving to Lane County. Sanford's mother, Sarah Cloyd Skinner, had crossed the Oregon Trail in 1877 with her family before they settled in the Willamette Valley. Sanford married Martha Ellen Kauble in 1878, and she died on June 9, 1882, in an awful accident from which she did not recover:

> *It appears that Mrs. Ellen Kauble was walking in a saw mill at that place and passing by a large wheel which was in motion had her veil caught in the cogs. Attempting to release it, her right arm was caught and crushed and ground between the cogs until it was badly lacerated. Medical assistance was called and the arm dressed, but on Thursday gangrene having set in an amputation was resorted to, the arm being taken off at the shoulder joint.*[22]

Hay forks on a northern Oregon farm. *Dorothea Lange, Farm Security Administration, Library of Congress.*

His second marriage, to Mary Emma "Emma" Richards, was in 1885. Their first child, Lena Skinner, was born on April 1, 1886, in Mohawk. They had a son, Cloyd Walter "Walter," Skinner on October 18, 1897. Sanford, Emma and their children lived in the home of Sarah Washburne, of a well-known pioneer family, for whom Sanford managed a large farm property.

Also living in the house was John Richards and his daughter, Edith. They had moved there to live with Mrs. Washburne after Richards divorced his wife. Nineteen-year-old Edith, one of John Richards's eight children, had moved in with her father from the home of her mother to visit and had arrived about two or three weeks before.

From all the coroner's report and newspaper articles on this matter, one can glean that there was some sort of family argument, possibly related to the Skinners' treatment of Edith. Sanford raised his objections about Edith to her grandmother, his mother-in-law, boss and landlord. He said that "if she stayed there he would move his family away."[23] Mrs. Washburne evidently preferred to keep her property manager and son-in-law on her property. As a consequence of the argument, Mrs. Washburne asked Edith to go to Frank Stafford's house, and she went there on the evening of Wednesday, May 31. Washburne gathered Edith's possessions together in a bundle either that night or early the next day.

At around 5:30 a.m. on June 1, 1905, Emma and Sanford rose as usual. Sanford prepared to run Edith's things over to where she had moved. He left through the front door and made it about thirty steps through the yard and to a small gate when he was suddenly shot in the back. The shot came from the upper-story window, where Richards had been lying in wait with a .45-caliber Winchester rifle. Sanford was found "lying in the gate in front of the house, with a large bullet hole through his body, the ball having entered the back and passed out through the abdomen, a wound from which he must have died in a very few moments."[24]

Richards then went after Emma, his sister. Emma tried to get away several times but led her brother one direction while her daughter escaped in the other direction. Emma most likely saved Lena in the process.

The coroner would later quote another resident of the home's perspective of the situation:

> *My name is David Albro. I reside with Sanford Skinner, am working for Mr. Skinner. My age is 33. I have been working for Mr. Skinner off and on for eight years.*
>
> *The body lying near the gate is Sanford Skinner....I was in bed when I heard a shot fired this morning. It was about 5 o'clock. The shot appeared to come from the south end of the house. I got up, dressed myself, and came out on the front porch. I met John Richards there; he had a rifle in his left hand and a revolver in his right hand. He said for me to get out of the way. I went out into the yard. He went back into the house.*[25]

Albro immediately went to the aid of Sanford Skinner. The tussle that happened next sounds as if it went by almost in fast-forward. Albro heard some shots fired an instant after Richards returned inside. When Albro reached Skinner, he was still alive.

Richards rushed out of the home, still holding the rifle, and gave it to Albro, saying to "take him over to Frank Stafford." Stafford, the nearby neighbor, was where Richards's daughter Ethel was staying. According to Richards, he "had some trouble with Skinner last evening."

The story Richards told Albro was that early the morning of the shootings, "he had been moving hay in the yard and Skinner went into the house and got her things, Ethel Richards'….Richards said that he shot them."[26]

The Skinners' nineteen-year-old daughter, Lena, told the coroner that she too was in bed when she heard a shot. What greeted her was a horror:

> *I was sleeping upstairs and came down stairs. I saw papa lying dead by the gate. John Richards was standing by the South door trying to load his revolver. Mama and I were standing together and he took after us. She went one way and I went another. The last I saw her she went around the corner and I was going up through the garden. I heard three shots fired, and I heard some afterwards, but I was too frightened to tell how many.*[27]

Lena ran barefoot through the yard and to the nearest neighbor, McGee, to both warn them and alert them to what had happened. She saw Richards and Albro on the way to the Stafford house and bravely ran back to her home to call Sheriff Fisk on the phone, give Richards's description and tell them to be on the lookout so Richards didn't escape from Lane County.

Sarah Washburn also gave her testimony about the events that day. She got up and was

> *in the house when John Skinner came into the house and said he wanted Ethel Richards' clothes. He gathered some of them up. He went out and I heard a shot fired, and then I saw John after Emma, and he shot her. The first shot came from upstairs. I talked to John and he said she abused his girl and scandalized her and it was more than he could stand.*

Lena S. Skinner Veatch gravestone, 2015. *Bob Wilson.*

Albro and Stafford were able to subdue Richards until the authorities came to arrest him. The coroner's jury found that John Richards was guilty of the murder of both John and Emma Skinner. The report revealed the gruesome details of how they died. Emma was shot "through the left wrist, through one leg, then shot through the body. As she lay on the stairway, Richard placed the old pistol to her head and blew her brains out."[28] Sanford Skinner, meanwhile, had one shot that entered his shoulder blade and came out though his chest. Both were assumed to have died quickly, if not instantly.

An interesting component of late 1800s–early 1900s criminology is the belief that you could study the bone structure of the face to determine criminality.[29] According to the *Morning Oregonian*,

> *Richards is a man about 50 years old, lank and lean, weighing about 120 pounds, dark complexion, sloping forehead, aquiline nose, and a decidedly vicious expression.*

Although questioned, Richards would say only that "they can hang me if they want to: the sooner, the better."[30] He was arraigned the day after the crime was committed and waived the right to be examined, thus being held on bail until he was to be tried in front of the circuit court, which would open on June 19, 1905.

The trial for having "murdered John [*sic*] Skinner by shooting him in the back and then turning on Skinner's Wife, Richards' own sister, and shooting her to death, blowing off the top of her head after she fell to the floor,"[31] was to start on June 27.

The evening before the trial was to begin, the grand jury filed its recommendation that the court accept a guilty charge of murder in the second degree instead of another charge, due to the circumstances around the killing—in other words, the nebulous claim Richards made of his daughter being mistreated. Accordingly, Richards withdrew his guilty plea of murder in the first degree and changed it to two counts of guilty of murder in the second degree. Richards agreed to waive time before being sentenced. Judge L.T. Harris sentenced him to life imprisonment in the Oregon state penitentiary. Richards remained impassive as the sentence was read.

The courtroom was virtually empty that day, since the public assumed Richards would be tried on his original trial date of the twenty-seventh. Word spread quickly outside, though, and "everybody expressed surprise," according to the *Plaindealer*, "as it was generally thought that the murderer would hang."

Cutting wood in winter, 1870. Print shows a snow-covered landscape with two men cutting wood on the edge of a country road, with a farmhouse in the background and pastures on the left. *William Herring, L. Prang & Co., Library of Congress.*

Much more must have been inferred by the general public of the day about what exactly went on to spur the killing spree. "Abuse and scandal," could mean sexual abuse, rough treatment, extreme expectations or exposure to something unsavory, according to the mores of the time. Evidently, more was shown to the jury, for the newspaper printed the grand jury's recommendation in total. Take note of the last sentence of the edict:

> *We, the Grand Jury, at the June, 1905 at the above court in the case of the state of* Oregon vs. John Richards, *referring to the indictment numbered "one," have to state from subsequent and additional evidence examined by us, the aforesaid indictment numbered "one," does an injustice to the above named defendant, John Richards, and we believe from all the evidence submitted that this grand jury cannot make out a case greater than murder in the second degree; nor should the defendant be convicted of a greater crime, it appearing to this grand jury, from all the evidence now before us, that the crime charged in said indictment numbered "one," was not committed in cool blood and that the killing was without deliberation or premeditation, and it appearing from information before us that the defendant, John Richards, is willing to enter a plea of guilty to the charge of murder in the second degree….*
>
> *We have examined into this matter with great care and make this recommendation after due deliberation. We fully realize the enormity of the defendant's crime and we also realize* the enormity of the provocation that caused him to commit the act [emphasis added].[32]

Richards went to jail and remained there until, after he had served some years of his sentence, he and some other "lifers," or those with life sentences, were pardoned by Governor Oswald West.

After their parents died, Lena Skinner raised her brother, Walter, who was eight years old at the time of the killings. She later married Harvey Veatch on November 30, 1905. Lena had a long life of service. She was "department president of the United Spanish War Veterans auxiliary" when she died and had previously been the "committee woman on the legislative committee of the auxiliary to the Veterans of Foreign Wars."[33] She had no children but doted on her nieces and nephews.

Her brother, Cloyd Walter Skinner, earlier known as Walter, had neither as long a life nor as peaceful an end. In another gruesome death to befall the family, he was killed in a horrific logging accident. Skinner and three other loggers were using dynamite to blow up tree stumps when one charge malfunctioned, and it exploded before it was supposed to go off. The three men were killed instantly on June 25, 1929; Walter was only thirty-one years old. Walter left three young children—Juanita, Lloyd and Walter Sanford—and a wife, Esther Renfro Skinner.[34]

3

"COME HELP ME"

Hermann and Lina Petersdorf

Hermann August Edward Petersdorf had been known to wake up his neighbors at odd times during the summer and fall of 1900. The farmer would get up in the wee hours of the morning or late at night to complain to them about all manner of things. Indeed, "Petersdorf had shown signs of insanity for three years," according to the newspaper.[35] However, the family did not know what to believe about his state of mind. His wife, Lina, was very pretty, to be certain, and kind and helpful—all in all, a good farmer's wife. No one knows Hermann's motives the night of September 18, 1900, when he woke up a nearby neighbor in the middle of the night, saying, "Come help me bury my wife." The story that follows is truly a tragedy that may have been prevented with our modern understanding of mental illness.

The Petersdorf family was of German descent and lived somewhere on High Pass Road between Eugene and Junction City, near an area where many other German and Scandinavian families had settled. Lina was thirty-one, and Herman was thirty-six. They had four children—Clara, Adolph, Elizabeth and Walter—ranging in age from seven years to four months old. Lina was an emigrant from Niederönz, Canton Bern, Switzerland, and she came to America in 1881 at age twelve with her brother and sister. Hermann August Edward Petersdorf hailed from Neu Schönwalde, Pommern, Prussia, present-day Zagozd, Poland.

Hermann was a veteran of the Prussian military. He and his sister Anna Albertine Henrietta Petersdorf Ragotzke came to the United States in 1890 or 1891. Lina's mother, Maria, had married Heinrich Fluckiger in

Hermann Petersdorf, 2016. *Joel Smith.*

Switzerland, and together they had daughters Maria Elise and Lina and sons Johann and Jakob. Jakob died, and then Heinrich died in 1873. Maria placed her younger kids with family and friends for safekeeping, and then she and young Maria Elise, known by family as "Lizzie," traveled to America in 1874 with her sister and brother-in-law to start anew and earn enough money to bring her other children over.[36] She worked as a maid during the winters, and her sister and brother-in-law's farm during the summers, and that's where she met her second husband Louis Schwader. They came to Nebraska to join her mother, Maria Rickli Schwaeder, her oldest sibling Maria, and her new stepfather. Lina and Hermann met near her mother's home in Nebraska, and they married in Dry Creek, Nebraska, on February 16, 1894.[37]

It's difficult today to imagine the near-complete darkness of the sky on the night of September 18, 1900, when Herman committed the murder of his wife. At ten or eleven o'clock, there were few constellations visible in the sky at the farm, northwest of Eugene and twelve miles from Junction City, where the Petersdorf family lived. Most farm equipment at that time was operated by oxen, donkey or person-power:

> *While some large farms had steam power, in the early 1900's many farmers were still using horses to power their threshing machines. From four to seven two-horse teams were used to turn the "power" mechanism, which was hooked to the thresher in the background by rotating iron rods.*[38]

There weren't store lights or security lights out in the country. It was truly dark. In a place where electric light was not commonly used outside, the farms were lit at night only by fires banked in each hearth each evening before residents went to bed. Lit electric arc lamps had only come to the territory in 1897 aboard the *State of California* steamship as it sailed into Portland.[39]

Imagine, then, how eerie it was on the night of September 17, 1900, when Hermann walked the dark half mile to the farm of his nearest neighbor, Frank Wilkinson, at what he thought was about eleven o'clock. "Come help me," he said. "Come help me bury my wife."

Frank Wilkinson told the coroner later that he was alarmed when:

> *Hermann Petersdorf came to my place last night about twelve o'clock and rapped and called to me and asked me to get up as he had killed his wife and wanted me to come and help bury her.*

He must have been stunned. Frank told Hermann "to go home and that he would be there in a short time." Hermann went home. Frank, after some quick thinking, retrieved neighbor John Moade and another neighbor, J.D. Cox, who was the county road supervisor, and together they went to the Petersdorf farm, where they found Hermann inside the house. By the time they got there, it was about 1:30 a.m.

> *He asked us if we were ready to dig that hole. He proposed that we get a box to bury her in. He went with us and showed us the body about thirty yards from the house by the fence. We then went after the lumber and notified the neighborhood. Mr. Cox and myself went to Junction and telegraphed the sheriff, and when I returned at 7:30 I found that Hermann Petersdorf was dead also.*[40]

John Moade concurred with the sequence of events laid out by Frank Wilkenson:

> *We found Petersdorf in the house; went with him to the place where the body of his wife lay; Petersdorf said that his wife tried to poison him and that his little girl told him not to drink the coffee because his wife had put poison in it.*

Moade had no idea why Petersdorf had become so violent toward his wife.

> *He lived here about four years. Last spring, a year ago, people in this neighborhood thought he was crazy. I also heard people this spring say that he was crazy. I never saw anything wrong with him.*[41]

Lina Petersdorf's father, Louis Schwader, lived about a quarter mile away. When he was questioned by the coroner, he said:

> *My son-in-law was at my house last Sunday and he was perfectly rational; I have known him about nine years and never knew anything wrong about him.*[42]

And yet, despite these assertions, the *Eugene Weekly Guard* stated that Hermann had "shown signs of insanity for about three years." Where is the disconnect? What was really going on with Hermann and Lina? And why did Hermann snap? And how could "his little girl," unnamed in the coroner's report, have possibly known that her mother, Lina, had poisoned the coffee? I would think that at 11:30 p.m., the children, all under the age of ten, would probably be asleep. We have no evidence or testimony otherwise except for Wilkerson's statement.

Many of the things said about Hermann were vague allusions, other than his penchant for late-night chats with neighbors. It seems possible that the newspapers took small amounts of information and inflated them for a more salacious story. One source said that Hermann "was of a sullen, morose disposition" and "of powerful physique" and "was considered a dangerous man."[43] Another source, and evidence from family members, suggests that he may have been dealing with a powerful mental illness, which was not treatable at the time and could account for much of Hermann's behavior.

Sheriff W.W. Withers described the crime scene when he arrived at about seven o'clock the following morning.

> [I] *found a crowd here ahead of me and found the woman about one hundred yards West of the house covered with fern; found that her face was all beat up, probably done with a club; her face was all covered with blood; I helped to remove her to the house and placed her on a lounge where she is now at the present time. I found the man lying dead on the floor in the sitting room with his head toward the fire-place; there were no marks of violence about his person.*[44]

Apparently, after Hermann committed the crime against his wife, he had dragged her into a small depression in the ground, laid down some ferns and partly covered her with more greenery. The description of her body in the newspapers was horrific:

> *The weapon used was a fir club about three feet long and about as thick as a man's arm. The murderer had evidently struck his victim seven or eight times. There was a gash over the woman's left eye through which the brains were oozing, her teeth were knocked loose, and forehead crushed in.*

The coroner attempted to create a timeline of the correct sequence of events. The interviews revealed that after showing his neighbors his wife's body, Hermann had come back to their house. Their daughter Clara told him not to drink a beverage made for him. She said his wife, Lina, had poisoned it. However, the evidence showed that Hermann's body was near a pail of water. The rim of the cup containing the beverage made for Hermann showed crystallized white powder, and the water inside, when tested, was shown to contain the poison strychnine. When the home was searched, investigators were able to produce a tiny vial that was full of the poison, and it was assumed this was where it had come from.[45]

Who put the strychnine in the glass, Lina or Hermann, was unclear. It seemed in many of the accounts to be heavily intimated that Lina was planning to poison Hermann, but more of the stories held Hermann alone responsible for both the murder of his wife and his own death. The timing suggests that he was.

Louis Schwader and his second wife, Lina's mother, Maria Rickli Schwader, took in the children to raise after the event. They lived next door. Lina's sister Bertha Schwader lived at home and helped raise the children as well.[46] A probate court announcement ran in the newspaper to that effect on October 6, 1900. An estate worth $500 at that time would be $18.591.19 in 2024, adjusted for inflation:

> *Probate Court.*
> *In the matter of the estate of Hermann Petersdorf, deceased. Petition for letters of administration. Probable value of the estate $500. Heirs are Clara, daughter aged 5 years, Adolf* [sic], *son aged three years, Walter, son aged four months, and a sister in Nebraska. J.D. Cox appointed administrator. Bonds $1000, Louis Schwader surety. Louis Schwader appointed guardian of minor heirs. Bond $1000, surety F.W. Williams.*[47]

This story is such a sad one. Unfortunately, the diagnosis and treatment of mental illness was absolutely not important from a societal sense at that time. It's entirely possible that Hermann was mentally ill, particularly if the neighbors' reports on his state of mind prior to the murder are accurate. Several newspapers speculated the reason behind the murder was despair, because the farm was possibly in great debt, but the inheritance the couple left makes that less likely, and there is no confirmation of such a debt. It's hard to guess why this happened and what could have prevented it. Perhaps Hermann just snapped, and acting rashly was the only way he could see through it.

The recognition of mental illness as a serious condition wasn't widespread in the United States until 1908, when Clifford Beers started the Connecticut Society for Mental Hygiene. Beers himself had bipolar disease and detailed his cruel treatment in mental institutions all over the country in his book, *A Mind That Found Itself*, which came out the same year. That organization later became the National Mental Health Association and is now called Mental Health America. It is "aimed at prevention, early intervention, and treatment."[48] The American Psychiatric Association didn't form a Joint Commission on Mental Illness and Health until the early 1950s.[49]

Hermann and Lina's great-grandson Joel Smith generously shared a huge amount of information about his family. Joel is the grandson of Clara Petersdorf Wolfe, Lina's oldest daughter. The murder/suicide was a near-forbidden subject within the family to his knowledge. After the tragedy, Clara, Adolph, Elizabeth and Walter continued to live with their maternal grandparents, who lived next door. Their aunt Bertha, Lina's sister, came to live with them and assumed care of the children as well. Joel said that they simply didn't talk about their great-grandparents much. "For the kids, they had to get on living," Joel said. "They were so young. It was like one day they were there, and the next day they were gone."

The kids stayed with their grandparents until they married or left home. Joel told me that family lore has it that Maria knew something was wrong on the morning of September 18, 1900, because there was no smoke coming from the cooking fire at her daughter's home, and Lina typically rose early to start the fire. Aunt Bertha stayed to take care of her parents, the farm and the children, and she never married. It was as if she'd had her kids already. "Aunt Bertha was their everything," Joel said. "They had a great love for her."

That love may have been why they didn't pry too much into Hermann and Lina's story, so as to not hurt their aunt. Joel was close to his great-grandmother Clara and his grandmother June. When Joel was young, he asked them about the family. Even at that young age, Joel was interested in family. He is the family historian today.

Bertha had a closed and locked trunk, he was told. "Bertha left instructions not to open the trunk until her death," Joel told me. After her death in 1974, her family opened it. It was the first time many of the descendants learned about the family tragedy of Lina and Hermann. It was full of newspaper articles, photos and even belongings of the couple. The event was a source of shame for the family, Joel explained to me. They didn't want to remember that it happened.

Joel learned a lot from his grandmother and great-grandmother. Clara's sister, Elizabeth, became a schoolteacher and married a man named Lynn Hayden Bailey in 1921. They lived in Monroe, Oregon, with their two children until her death in 1989. Clara's uncle Charles Schwader married late and never had children. Clara's brother Adolph was a longtime logger and married his wife, Cecile, in 1923. They had three children, twelve grandchildren and nine great-grandchildren. Adolph found their parents had no grave markers in the late 1970s, so he paid to have gravestones made for them in the High Pass Cemetery.

The Schwader farm was kept in the family. Adolph bought out all the other siblings and lived there himself. Walter was a hook tender for a logging company and was unfortunately crushed by a log in 1951.

Clara Johanna Henrietta Petersdorf Wolfe married Ervin Monroe Wolfe in 1916, and they had seven children, fourteen grandchildren and twelve great-grandchildren. They'd met after the Wolfe family advertised for someone to look after their aging mother, and Clara got the job. She was very shy. Joel recalled her as someone who "would never cuss. The worst thing she'd ever say was, 'Oh, sugar!' There wasn't a mean bone in her body." Clara had long hair, even into her eighties, and had a braid that she would take down every night.[50]

She never wore pants and was most comfortable with older things. She lived in a circa 1890s home with a wooden sink on the back porch and cooked every meal on a wood-fired stove. "Clara was the favorite," Joel joked with me. "She was the only one who had two middle names!" She was talented at tatting and embroidery and taught her daughter June. June framed a pillowcase that the two of them made to give to Joel, and he treasures the connection.

Joel shared his personal conviction that there was no premeditation on Hermann's part when he killed Lina. He believes that Hermann probably killed Lina and then killed himself on realizing the magnitude of what he had done. "I just want to continue the conversation about mental illness," Joel said. "Out of darkness always comes a little bit of light, and we're now so much more compassionate of victims and even murderers. Hermann did something horrible, and I don't want to minimize her suffering. But, her children were successful. They made it; not only did they have families, but they were genuinely happy inside."

Joel Petersdorf was immensely helpful in ferreting out the real story of the Petersdorf tragedy. He found and shared some paperwork regarding the sale of the property Hermann and Lina lived on. Based on that and some deed

Right: Family photo of Clara Petersdorf Wolfe. *Joel Smith.*

Below: The Ford Century Farm on Doane Road is over 150 years old. This is not the Petersdorf farm but a location that appears much like the Petersdorf farm would have at the time of the tragedies. *Gary Halvorson, Oregon State Archives.*

translation help from Robin Meyers at the Lane County History Museum, the rough location of the original property was found. No homestead remains, and their graves are on private property so are not visible to the general public. Even on a sunny day in the bucolic countryside, it is easy to imagine the isolation of the place on a dark night long ago.

4

DEATH BY DONKEY ENGINE

Misadventure in the Logging Camps and Mills of Eugene

Naturally, in a place like Oregon, the trees that surround the valley are an abundant and renewable resource that residents need. Eugene "in the early 1850s connected two sloughs off the Willamette River, creating a millrace that ran through town to power grist mills and sawmills." Mills and wood product–related businesses grew as the population did, and the *Oregon Encyclopedia* reports that "by the mid-twentieth century, almost half of Lane County's workforce of 56,000 was employed in lumber-related jobs."[51]

Of all the ways to die in the early years of Eugene, logging accidents were one of the most difficult ways to go.

Take this one for example:

> *The men were at work with a donkey engine hauling logs and instead of all following the same track, occasionally a log would slide behind a tree, making it necessary to unfasten the chain and take a new hitch. One had just been caught in this way and (Joseph) Lloyd, accompanied by the hook tender, went to it for the purpose of loosening it. The other men noticed that the tree around which the chain was wrapped, was falling; and shouted to warn Lloyd and his companion. The latter lay down beside the log and was unhurt, but Lloyd, attempting to run out of the way of danger, was caught by the tree and instantly killed.*[52]

Timber work was one of the most important industries in the success of the Pacific Northwest. Timber work was "the wheel which sets all other wheels

Donkey engine on skids, 1941. This engine provides power for lumbering operations, and the skids make for easy transportation in the woods. *Russell Lee, Farm Security Administration, Library of Congress.*

in motion"[53] and has been a primary source for work since the state began. Frederic Weyerhaeuser was one of the East Coast lumbermen who bought up large tracts of land in the Northwest for timber sales in the late 1800s–early 1900s, and many of those lumber sites and the Weyerhaeuser mill can still be seen today near Eugene. The advent of the railroad led to more logging in higher elevations by the 1880s. Single bitted axes gave way over time to two-man crosscut saws, double-bitted axes and then the steam donkey engine.

A donkey engine worked like this:

> *In the simplest logging setup, a "line horse" would carry the cable out to a log where its tree had been downed. The cable would be attached, and, on signal, the donkey's operator (an engineer) would open the regulator, allowing the steam donkey to drag, or "skid," the log towards it. The log was taken either to a mill or to a "landing," where it would be transferred for onward shipment by railroad, road or river—either send down a flume, loaded onto boats, or floated directly in the water, often becoming part of a large log raft or "boom." Later, a "haulback" drum was added to the*

> *donkey, where a smaller cable could be routed around the "setting" and connected to the end of the heavier "mainline" to replace the line horse.*[54]

Basically, the donkey engine made logging easier by pulling the lines and yarding the lumber at the cutting site. Inherent dangers existed with all its moving parts, as well as with the team of animals (oxen, horses) and sled that carried the equipment. It was a benefit of the Industrial Revolution.

One tragic day, fifteen-year-old Charles Holt met his end by the implements of modern logging. An employee of the Booth-Kelly Lumber Company, Charles often perched on top of the wagon as it went down its path to the pond. "It is presumed that the horse started suddenly, the boy slipped and fell, and the sled ran onto his body in which condition it was found," said the *Eugene Weekly Guard*. Several personal accounts of the incident were included in the coroner's report, and though subtly different, all told the gruesome tale. Archie King wrote in his testimony:

> *I am the engineer for the donkey engine. I was at Eugene, about 800 feet from where the accident happened. Heard a yelling and went to see what was the matter. On arriving at the scene of the accident, I found boy—Chas Holt—under the water sled. Helped to pull boy from under sled. Think sled would be about 700 pounds. Sled was full of water. Boy was returning from spring…He was found about 20 minutes after he left with donkey engine for water.*[55]

The attending physician, N.L. Cheshire, wrote of Holt's injuries that "I found the body very cyanotic generally," and that there were "extrusions on both the right and left sides of the body" in a diagonal stripe from the left chest to the right upper shoulder, though Charles had no broken bones. His final pronouncement was that "death was probably due to direct stoppage of the heart by compression due to the great pressure on the chest."[56]

Archie King, who must have been distraught, also remarked in his testimony that Charles, who was generally dour, was used to going by himself with the horse to get water. The boy commonly sat on a burlap or cotton sack on top of the apparatus:

> *The sack was found about 30 feet behind where the accident happened. I think the boy was dead when I reached him. His hat was also found near the sack. The horse was hitched to the sled and standing quietly when the boy was found.*[57]

The fireman for the donkey engine, Robert Brown, confirmed the doctor's placement of the sled on young Charles. The subtext reveals the shock that might have swept through the logging camp as they tried to help the boy.

> *His head and arms were to the right of right-hand runner. His feet and body were between the runners under the sled. The right runner was diagonally over his chest. After we took him from under the sled, we carried him to the spring, where we put water on his face, thinking we might bring him back to life.*[58]

The Booth-Kelly Lumber Company was the site of another gruesome injury just a couple of years later. E.S. "Dock" Anders, forty-five, worked on the side of the river at the sawmill, and his job was to bring up the logs to place on the sawmill ramp. Anders, who was well thought of in the community, was a member of fraternal organizations like the Woodsmen of the World and the Odd Fellows. He and his wife had three children. On the day of his accident, he was working as usual pulling up logs:

> *It seems that the "dog"* [metal staple] *had not been driven into the logs securely, and flying out, struck the man on the left temple with such force as to shatter the skull, scattering his brains in every direction. He lived only a few minutes after the accident. Immediately after the accident Dr. R.G. Van Valsah was sent for, but for some reason he refused to go. Dr. W. Kueykendall was then telephoned for and left immediately but arrived after death had come.*[59]

Mill work was equally as dangerous as a profession in the early part of the 1900s. James Moore, a foreman of a mill near Barger in Eugene, died in a terrible and rare accident. When logs were harvested, often the workers would float them down the river as the fastest and easiest way to transport them to the sawmill to prepare for their journey to the marketplace.

Moore was in the process of "driving" a giant raft of logs in the McKenzie River near the Coburg section of Eugene. He stood on top of the middle of a section of logs in the middle of the raft to guide them along. Moore was knocking and kicking the "log dogs," or the giant metal staple-like pinchers that held the logs together. On a particularly large log, he misjudged the depth of the water in the process of knocking out the "dogs" that held the raft in a stack. Suddenly, he stepped off the logs just as the river moved into a section that was much faster and deeper than before. Moore fell in. His struggle to survive was watched by all who were present, sadly:

Massive log raft on the Columbia River, 1906. This is a good example of how giant logs were transported to the mills and further production. *Brück & Sohn Kunstverlag, Library of Congress.*

> *He was at once taken off his feet by the swift current and rapidly borne downstream. He floated perhaps 100 yards when he sank, but shortly afterwards came to the surface and floated again quite a distance. Samuel Garrison and young son were fishing near there and saw the unfortunate man being carried to his death.*
>
> *Mr. Moore saw them, and shouted for help, but it was impossible to do anything for him as the river was full of logs and the water was exceedingly swift.... Seeing that he could not be saved, Mr. Moore gave up and cried, "I am gone!" At this moment he reached a whirlpool and was drawn under, never to come to the surface again alive.*[60]

A person was in danger working in any form of logging at that time, and there wasn't much that could be done about it. James Holce was killed by a log while he was dragging it to the river in 1900. His companions noted that the trip, which generally took the man and his horse about fifteen minutes, had stretched to over an hour by the time they thought to look. Holce had been "banking" the twenty-four-foot-long, twenty-four-inch-diameter log—that is, placing it parallel to other logs in a stack near the river before they were ready for the "drive" or float down the river to the sawmill.

Willamette River log raft, 1973. This was often the most efficient way to transport logs and is still used today. *David Falconer, U.S. National Archives and Records Administration.*

> *They found Holce prostrate on the ground at the river bank with the log across his back….No one saw the accident, but the theory is advanced that as Holce swang into the banking place at an angle, the swinging of the log caused it to roll, and he probably stumbled, or was not aware of the rolling log until caught. The log rolled over his legs and body across the neck where it was held from rolling further by his head. Of course the unfortunate man hardly knew what hurt him, as a log of that size weighs not less than four thousand pounds.*[61]

It was so hard to get the log off of the unfortunate Holce that the crew had to roll it back over him, and they mentioned the sound of his bones crunching as they did so, but they simply had no other means of getting him free of the heavy weight. His coroner's report stated, "The blood is oozing from both ears….Death was most likely caused by direct compression, stopping both the circulation and respiration."[62]

Sawmills operated on long shifts. Ten-hour days were common, and the men lived crammed together in camps that later became "company towns" in a lot of cases. The company town model was deceptive, in that the company built places for workers and their families to live, but you had to rent them. Of course, there was also a store, purchases from which conveniently came off your paycheck. Their brutal lifestyle included fighting, gambling and a lot of drinking. Author Daniel DeMay wrote in an article for SeattlePI that his grandfather, a former logger, was so conditioned to the violence that one morning, when his wife came to wake him up for breakfast she surprised him, and he "knocked her out cold."[63]

Home logging operations were especially dangerous. In a horrible turn of events, twelve-year-old Joe Willis and his brother were felling trees on their parents' property in Eugene in 1901. The two boys worked in tandem to cut the timber, with a system of one steadying the tree while the other one chopped and took turns that way. That morning, Joe

> *placed his hand on the tree and looked to see which way it was going to fall, when his brother, not seeing the hand, struck it with the ax, making a fearful wound. The doctors found it necessary to take off the last two fingers and part of the hand, which was the right.*[64]

As the late 1800s became the 1900s, technological advances came slowly to transform the industry. Horse-drawn machines were replaced by steam-powered ones, and deforestation came at a more rapid pace as loggers were

Logger's garb. Wooden sculpture depicting typical loggers' gear at the Collier Logging Museum at Collier State Park in Chiloquin, Oregon, 2018. *Carol M. Highsmith, Library of Congress, Prints & Photographs Division.*

able to cut more board-feet of timber. The response times, accessibility issues in the remote areas and medicine grew as well, and logging is much safer today, although it is still the most dangerous job to have in America as of this writing, according to the annual *Forbes* magazine's "10 Most Dangerous Jobs" list.[65]

5

ILLUMINATION OF DANGER

Clifton Shriver

The city of Eugene was ready for advancements to make life easier and to get the streets lit up. "In the aftermath of a 1906 outbreak of typhoid fever in Eugene, which was traced to poor operating conditions at the privately owned water utility," explained the Oregon Historical Society, "the city sought to ensure its residents clean, reliable drinking water."[66] The unhygienic conditions sickened many, with deaths not uncommon. It was dark, besides, and the new streets and street corners needed visibility.

As such, the town residents sought to create an entity to bring clean water and reliable electricity. With the bond money from measures passed in 1908 and 1911, the voters made the Eugene Water Board and bought water pumps to serve them via an electric utility. The organization would eventually become the Eugene Water and Electric Board (EWEB) in 1949, still in operation today.[67]

The demand for new, labor-saving items grew through the early 1900s. Imagine having an electric iron when previous efforts had you placing the solid irons in the coals or on a stovetop to heat, or the convenience of having an electric carpet sweeper as opposed to sweeping up many times a day by hand. An electric franchise was granted to the Eugene Electric Company on February 14, 1887. The private company's 100-horsepower generating plant was direct-current type and placed on East Seventh and Ferry Streets in downtown Eugene. Later in 1897, the horsepower went up to 240.[68] By the 1880s, the "Brush" or "arc" electric lights were common in city areas across America. They gave off harsh lighting that was said to be nearly two

Early electric vacuum cleaner by Electric Suction Sweeper Company, circa 1908, predecessor of Hoover vacuum cleaner (1922). Exhibit in National Museum of American History, Washington, D.C., 2011. *Daderot, own collection.*

hundred times stronger than incandescent light bulbs, which was perfect for illuminating city squares.[69]

On December 31, 1892, some young people were out walking on the sidewalk of Eugene. They were having fun and in "a playful mood," according to one of the young men present, twenty-one-year-old Otto Gilstrap. Clifton Stevens, seventeen years and twenty-six days old, was in the lead. Frank Wilkins, sixteen; Lottie Johnson, seventeen; Celia Loomis, seventeen; and Lottie's little brother, who was nine or ten, were also in the group.

All said in their later statements that they were having a nice evening and just having a good time. Then, as Lottie Johnson said, things took a drastic turn when Clifton ran behind the group:

> *We were coming along when deceased said, "I'll take a swing," and grabbed the wire with both hands and threw his weight on it; next I saw he seemed to be off the ground, but I am not certain as to that; he said, "Boys, take me off!" We all ran to him. He fell on the ground on his back, his feet near the pole. He shook the arc and I heard it rattle like chains going together. He seemed to be in agony, his hands were clenched and together, one immediately above the other as he held the wire. After the shock and as he lay on the ground his hands were in front of him.*[70]

Otto Gilstrap concurred. He had been the first to reach his friend after the accident.

> *I was with the deceased 15 minutes before twelve on the night of December 31, 1892. I was in front of him and put my hand on the iron windlass* [pulley or mechanics used to suspend the light]. *I heard him say nothing, but he ran and grabbed the wire running up the pole from the spool with both hands and jerked it out from the pole, and as he did so I heard the arc light above rattle.*

It's difficult to imagine how scared and frightened the group must have been. Electricity, while not unknown, wasn't so ubiquitous as to be commonplace, and deaths due to it must have been rare at best. The sight was at once gruesome and pitiable, as Otto Gilstrap continued:

> *He said immediately, "Boys, come pull me away," and I went to him at once, turning back to him, having gone on about 30 feet past where*

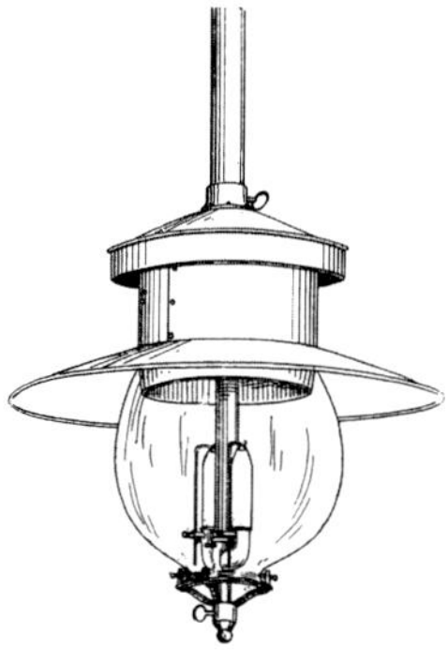

Lichfield 1000 Candle Power Outdoor Arc Light. An outdoor arc light, often suspended in the air, 1905. *Anonymous, Catalogue of the Litchfield Lamp Manufacturing Company.*

it occurred; he was lying on the ground with his feet about two feet from the pole. He was lying naturally and as we took hold of him he was very limp. We placed him on the sidewalk and I saw burns on the inside of both his hands; the skin was broken.... The hands of the deceased let go and he fell when he uttered the exclamation; I experienced no shock when I took hold of the spool. I touched the coil of wire as well as the spool.

He took hold of the wire directly in front of his body and his hands and arms were horizontal. I think the spool was about the height of his head; he was in a playful mood; he did not brace his feet on the pole; I am not certain that he ran to the pole, but playfully took hold of it. There was no talk there about the wires or about any danger.

Lottie Harris described the immediate aftermath of the terrible event:

> *After the shock and as he was laying on the ground his hands were in front of him. I was rubbing his forehead as he lay on the sidewalk and he said, "My God!," in a hoarse whisper. He breathed four or five natural, heavy sighs after he exclaimed, "My God!" I was ahead of him when he took hold of the wire. The lamp clinked twice I am certain, and I think as many as three times.*[71]

Dr. T.W. Harris was called for immediately. When he got there, Clifton was dead, but Harris was compelled to give what lifesaving measures he could. His coroner's testimony read:

> *I felt for his pulse and found none; I found that his heart had ceased to beat. I employed artificial respiration hoping to restore the action of the heart, but all without avail; I tried this for about five to ten minutes. I decided further effort was useless.*[72]

One interesting component of the coroner's thorough report was that it included a statement from the manager of the electric company, Charles Williams. The testimony, also published in the newspaper, gives a more accurate account of what the light looked like and the mechanics of how Shriver died.

> *The lamp is hung on a patent hanger by a horizontal wood bar with a porcelain insulator on the end of the bar. The top of the lamp has six or seven inches below this bar, and the bar hangs in clutches of the patent hangers so that when the lamp is hanging free there is six or seven inches of air space between top of lamp and any metal connection that could be made to reach the wire that connects with the spool on the pole.*
>
> *A shock could only be received by pulling down on the flexible wire lamp cord till lamp is raised so that top of lamp touches bottom of the clutch, then the current would pass from top of lamp to the iron clutch, from clutch to the iron pulley and thence to wire lamp cord and down to the person holding same and through his body.*[73]

Williams went on to describe the unfortunate perfect storm of movements that led to Stevens's death from a mechanical standpoint.

> *The lamps weigh between 45 and 50 pounds and I think the pull would have to be between 70 to 75 pounds to pull the lamp up to a connection. It wouldn't matter whether force was applied by side jerk or downward.... At that time of night he would have received about 1500 volts as the commercial lights were shut off.*

Electric Company Superintendent J.F. Robinson, Williams's boss, said that the city had required the electric company to place the streetlights at the intersections. The electric company had had issues with the lights coming down several times and had fixed the lamps by tying up with ropes, but he had notified the city that it was dangerous "This is the first instance I've ever heard of this kind," Robinson said. "I considered it absolutely safe."

As a result of this case, the city of Eugene heeded that verdict of the coroner's inquest. The final recommendation was that the Eugene Electric Company "raise the spools attached to the light poles to a height of eight feet from the ground to the bottom of the spool." In this way, Clifton Stevens's death served as a means to make things safer for the industry in both Eugene and later in the rest of the state when other electric companies followed suit.

One of the saddest parts of this story is the obituary. Stevens and his family had moved to Eugene from Minneapolis, Minnesota, three years before he died. He had four brothers and two sisters at the time of his death.

He was a sophomore at the State College, "in which he always stood among the foremost," and served as the exchange and educational editor at the university publication *The Reflector*. His parents and friends spoke of his "noble manner, genial goodwill, and straight-forward manliness."

Given that it was the last day of the year, the group of young people had a long conversation earlier in the evening about their lives and about death as they strolled together. In a weird premonition before his death, Stevens wrote and quoted to his friends the following, which they later wrote down:

Here lies his head upon the lap of earth,
A youth to fortune and fame unknown,
Fair science frowned not on his humble birth
And melancholy marked him for her own.

Large was his bounty and his soul since
Heaven did recompense largely send;
He gave to misery (all he had) a tear;
He gained from Heaven (t'was all he wished) a friend.

No further think his merits to disclose
Or draw his frailties from their dread abode;
(There they alike in trembling hope repose)
The bosom of his Father and his God.[74]

6
THEFT AND LAW ENFORCEMENT

Henry J. Day

It comes as a startling surprise to Sherriff Withers and the people of Lane County that Henry J. Day, first deputy sheriff, is a defaulter in the sum of $2,110.49, and that his whereabouts are unknown.[75]

Sheriff Withers, mentioned in detail elsewhere in this book, was extremely confident in Day, his first deputy and the office bookkeeper. In the time before the crime occurred, Day had proved himself indispensable to the sheriff in doing the paperwork and organizational side of the office, as Withers had been very busy investigating crimes and doing work in places far and near.

Henry J. Day was from Lane County. His parents, George Byrn Day and Amelia (Smelling) Day, traveled over the Oregon Trail in 1852 to first settle in Camp Creek, Oregon. He was born in Lane County, Oregon, in 1860. He had eleven siblings, of whom he was the oldest. He and his family were some of the earliest immigrants to the area, and they were considered an honorable pioneer family. At twenty-two, he married Julia Catherine Goodman, and the two had three children together. Day was generally well-liked and "held in the highest esteem by his many friends." His father, the Reverend George B. Day, and his brother Reverend F.J. Day were mentioned in the newspapers as being prominent Baptist pastors. Henry J. Day was the assistant fire chief for the city of Eugene as well.

Part of what made people so incredulous about the theft was the fact that Henry J. Day was historically an individual who cherished and was a

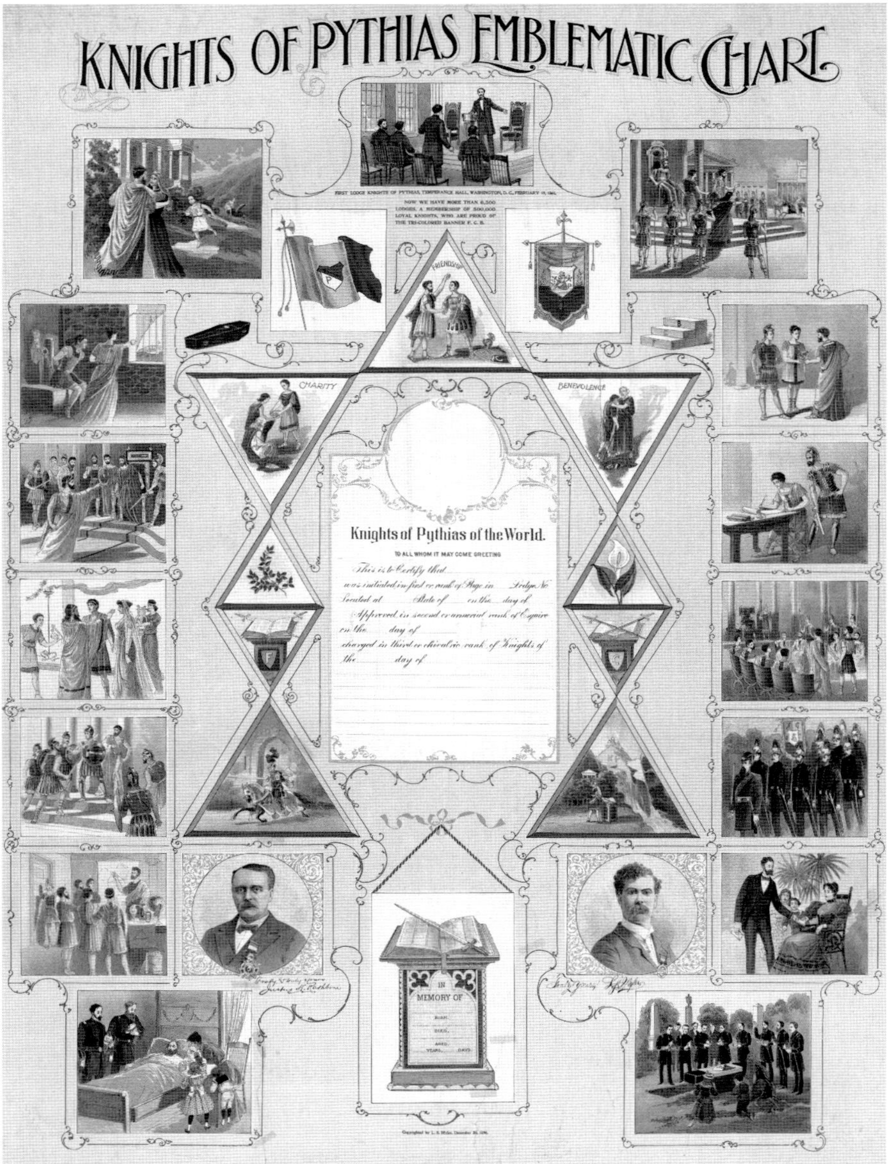

Knights of Pythias emblematic chart, 1897. *Library of Congress.*

dedicated member of his community. Before he was a deputy sheriff, he served multiple terms as city marshal. As a Union Party member, he was the chairman of their Lane County central committee. Several fraternal societies in the area counted him as a long-standing member. They included the Native Sons, the Woodsmen of the World, the AF&AM organization and the Knights of Pythias, an organization dedicated to benevolence, friendship and charity.[76] In short, nobody could fathom why he had stolen the money.

Only a few years before, in 1894, a newspaper's gossipy "Items," section, as things seen about town were called, was quoted as saying that "Henry J. Day is certain to be Eugene's next sheriff. He will make an excellent officer."[77]

After the theft was discovered, Sheriff Withers, who was quoted as most "regretful," told all that he would make the debt good himself. He spent his own money to do so and was dogged in his search for the missing man and the missing money. Withers, County Judge Potter and Deputy District Attorney Harris put up a countywide one-hundred-dollar reward for Day's arrest and detention.

The November 4, 1889 edition of the *Eugene City Guard* extolled the sheriff in this matter, which appears to have caused embarrassment and shame to him so that he made it right for the community.

> *"The Sheriff of Lane County announces that he will make good the shortage of his defaulting and absconding deputy, H.J. Day. This is right and honorable."*
>
> *The above extract is from the editorial columns of Sunday's* Salem Statesman. *It is a novelty in Oregon, when the public officer defaults, and especially so if the dishonest man be a deputy, for the county to receive all monies due without long and expensive litigation.*[78]

The sheriff paid the full amount that Day stole back to the county within twenty-four hours. However, doing that meant that he would not take a payment for his work for a period of two years. The action also put his small farm at risk. The *Guard* article ended by saying, "Every voter in Lane County sympathizes with Mr. Withers in his loss of dollars and betrayal of trust."

An editorial in the same issue of the *Eugene City Guard*, November 4, 1899, revealed the community's deep sadness after the theft:

> *A Sad Betrayal of Trust.*
>
> *It is the unexpected that often happens. That Henry J. Day should have proved faithless to the trust reposed in him is as if the writer had been struck a cruel blow in the face by a trusted friend. We have known him*

intimately for many years—socially, politically, fraternally, in business relations—and can say that in all these years, we never knew of his doing a dishonorable act, or even making a dishonorable suggestion.[79]

Henry J. Day disappeared. He was seen four years later in Comstock, California. By a stroke of luck, Henry W. Stewart, who worked as an agent at the Southern Pacific Railroad in California, recognized Day as he boarded the train. Stewart had been born and raised in Springfield, and the newspaper called him "thoroughly reliable." He wrote his experience in a letter sent to the Eugene Police Department.

While at the Southern Pacific Train depot here last night at 11 o'clock, I came face to face with Henry J. Day, the ex-deputy Sheriff of Lane County, who suddenly dropped out of sight several years ago, leaving the late Sheriff Withers to make good a deficit of about two thousand dollars on account of his crooked work.

When he recognised me, he turned quickly and walked down in front of the depot parcel room. To make doubly sure, I followed him at a rapid pace, and as he turned about I looked him fully in the face. He gave me a startled stare, quickly turned and boarded the train that was standing in the yard almost ready to pull out for Reno, Nevada, and Odgen, Utah. After boarding the train he took a seat at the furthest side of the car from the platform, pulled his hat well down over his face, remaining in that position until the train pulled out. My wife was with me and noted it all.

I could see little or no change in his appearance from what it was when he left Eugene several years ago.[80]

Sadly, that was the last that was ever seen of Henry J. Day, disgraced policeman and fireman. He was sought for in vain but was never caught. Or so it was thought. The records went dry for Henry J. Day after that sighting in California. However, a match with several genealogical sites to one Henry "Jackson" Day, also known simply as Jackson Day, shows a strong possibility about what happened. A man of that name appeared, or reappeared, in Lane County decades later.

Jackson Day has the same birth date, death date, parents and siblings as Henry Jackson Day. Jackson shares the same first wife, Julia, and the same children. Julia and Henry J. Day had their first daughter, Estelle "Stella" Day, in 1883. Their second daughter, Lena Day, followed in 1890. Their son, Clarke H. Day, was born in 1892.

Southern Pacific Railroad Cutoff, Tunnel No. 18. 1909. *Historic American Engineering Record, Library of Congress.*

Southern Pacific Railroad Station, 1978. *William A. Wilson, Paradise Valley Folklife Project Collection (AFC 1991/021).*

There was an intriguing gap between the times he was proven by records to be a resident in Lane County.

If the theft that Henry J. Day committed was in 1899, where did he go before he reappeared with the new name? One clue might be the sighting outside of Sacramento at the Comstock Station. The witness said that he was taking the train that was going to Nevada and then on to Utah. Further questioning found that the witness had Henry J. Day on the train going the farthest distance away from the station they were at. We know where he went toward, but not why or if it really was he who came back.

Lizzie Anderson Forrest married Jackson Day on September 2, 1926, in Lane County. Lizzie Anderson had adopted a daughter, Ethlyn Forrest, with her first husband, Civil War veteran Leman Forrest, in 1902, and it appears that Jackson did not adopt her after the marriage, as she would have been an adult and married herself at the time, but Ethlyn is counted as a caring stepdaughter in his obituary.

Is it possible that twenty-five years later, by the time he returned to Eugene, Henry's theft had been forgotten? The debt had been paid, after all, by Sheriff W.W. Withers, before his unfortunate death in 1903, so it could have been a moot point. A record of Henry's divorce from Julia was hard to find, but evidently the divorce did occur, sometime during the period when he was gone. Henry Jackson Day died on November 4, 1927. He and Lizzie had been married for the short span of fourteen months. No record of a connection between the two men was publicly printed, in any case, until his obituary.

Henry's obituary reads:

> *HENRY J. DAY IS DEAD*
>
> *MEMBER OF PIONEER FAMILY PASSES AT 67*
>
> *Henry J. Day, member of a pioneer family, died at his home at 1211 High Street yesterday at the age of 67 years.*
>
> *Mr. Day was an early-day deputy sheriff of Lane County and had lived in Eugene a greater part of his life. He is survived by his widow, Mrs. Elizabeth Day, one son, Clark Day, of Salem, one step-daughter, Ethlyn Forrest of Eugene, three grandchildren, Juanita Kilbourne and Gerald and Doris Day, and four brothers and sisters.*[81]

Stella Day, his daughter from his first marriage, had died in 1910 of pneumonia. She had been sick for a few years, but not bedridden until the last several weeks she was alive. Her father, Henry Jackson Day, was not named in Stella's obituary, even though he would still have been living. There is no evidence of the reason why, but one can guess that his divorce of her mother, or the disgrace of his theft and abandonment, may have been the cause. Her sister and Henry's second daughter, Lena (Day) Kilborne, died a year after her sister in 1911.

Through careful perusal of the documents available, there was no other trace of Henry J. Day, or Henry "Jackson" Day. All the details matched up; the two men had to be the same, but there was no connecting thread. Jan and Mike, people who have kindly posted a lot of information regarding Lane County residents on genealogical sites, shared much information about Henry Jackson Day. In an inquiry as to whether the two men were one and the same, Jan responded:

> *My family research had focused on the Gillespie side of Lane County Pioneers, through Rev. Jacob Gillespie. I only have limited information regarding Henry Jackson Day, but I do believe this is the same man you are referring to in your note.*
>
> *Henry Jackson Day was the grand-nephew of Rev. Jacob Gillespie. When Rev. Gillespie led a wagon train from Missouri in 1852, he brought many family members and neighbors with him, including Henry Jackson Day's father George B. Day. These friends and neighbors were looking for greener pastures due to the drought in Missouri in the 1850's so this at least partially explains why so many people were migrating west.*
>
> *Yes, I have seen the newspaper stories of the Day Embezzlement. I found nothing to explain what happened after William W. Withers replaced the missing monies or where Day fled to after leaving Lane County. The connection, which you are likely aware of, is that Henry Jackson Day and Sheriff Withers were second cousins.*

Jan went on to explain:

> *Withers was a grandson of Sheriff Gillespie and Lane County was a very small place at the time. So, it was Withers' professional as well as family honor that was at stake. In the newspaper reports, at least some people criticized Withers for hiring Day in the first place and for Withers not making sure the financial accounts were audited daily.*

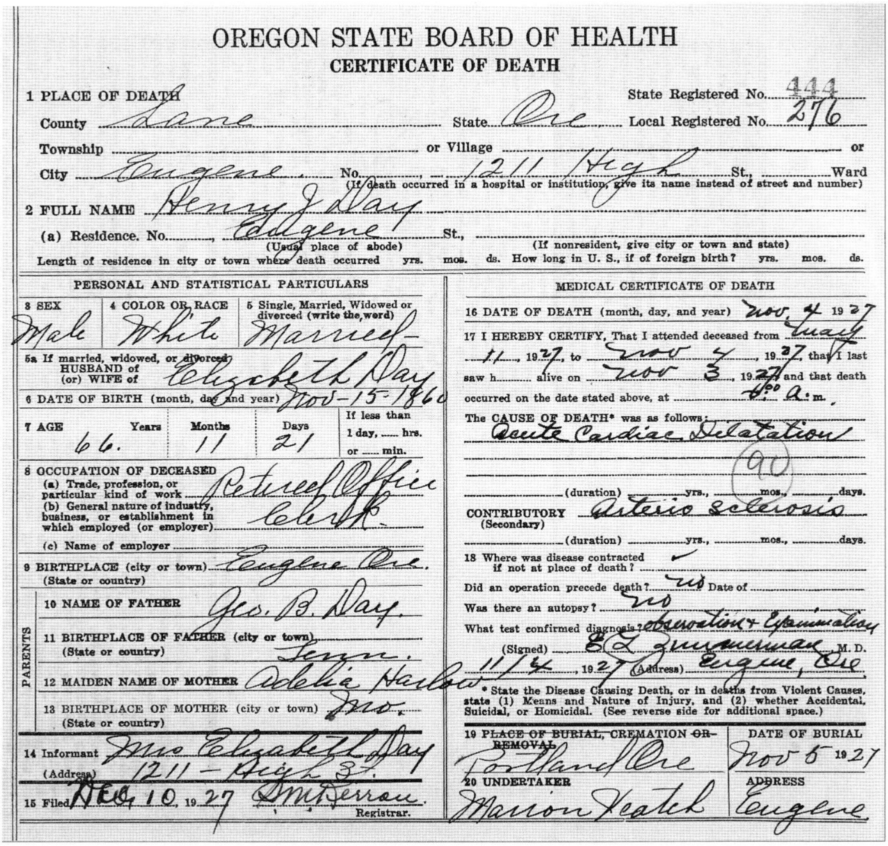

OREGON STATE BOARD OF HEALTH
CERTIFICATE OF DEATH

1 PLACE OF DEATH
County Lane State Ore State Registered No. 444
Local Registered No. 276
Township .... or Village .... or
City Eugene No. 1211 High St., ... Ward
(If death occurred in a hospital or institution, give its name instead of street and number)

2 FULL NAME Henry J Day
(a) Residence. No. .... Eugene St., ...
(Usual place of abode) (If nonresident, give city or town and state)
Length of residence in city or town where death occurred yrs. mos. ds. How long in U. S., if of foreign birth? yrs. mos. ds.

PERSONAL AND STATISTICAL PARTICULARS

3 SEX Male
4 COLOR OR RACE White
5 Single, Married, Widowed or divorced (write the word) Married
5a If married, widowed, or divorced HUSBAND of (or) WIFE of Elizabeth L Day
6 DATE OF BIRTH (month, day and year) Nov-15-1860
7 AGE Years 66. Months 11 Days 21 If less than 1 day, ... hrs. or ..... min.
8 OCCUPATION OF DECEASED
(a) Trade, profession, or particular kind of work Retired Office
(b) General nature of industry, business, or establishment in which employed (or employer) Clerk
(c) Name of employer
9 BIRTHPLACE (city or town) (State or country) Eugene Ore.

PARENTS
10 NAME OF FATHER Geo. B. Day
11 BIRTHPLACE OF FATHER (city or town) (State or country) Tenn.
12 MAIDEN NAME OF MOTHER Adelia Harlow
13 BIRTHPLACE OF MOTHER (city or town) (State or country) Mo.

14 Informant Mrs Elizabeth L Day
(Address) 1211 - High St.
15 Filed Dec 10, 1927 [illegible] Registrar.

MEDICAL CERTIFICATE OF DEATH

16 DATE OF DEATH (month, day, and year) Nov. 4 1927
17 I HEREBY CERTIFY, That I attended deceased from [illegible] 11, 1927, to Nov 4, 1927, that I last saw h..... alive on Nov 3, 1927 and that death occurred on the date stated above, at 4:00 a.m.
The CAUSE OF DEATH* was as follows:
Acute Cardiac Dilatation
(90)
(duration) ..... yrs., ... mos., ... days.
CONTRIBUTORY (Secondary) Arterio sclerosis
(duration) ..... yrs., ... mos., ... days.
18 Where was disease contracted if not at place of death?
Did an operation precede death? no Date of
Was there an autopsy? no
What test confirmed diagnosis? Observation & Examination
(Signed) E L [illegible] M.D.
11/4, 1927 (Address) Eugene, Ore
*State the Disease Causing Death, or in deaths from Violent Causes, state (1) Means and Nature of Injury, and (2) whether Accidental, Suicidal, or Homicidal. (See reverse side for additional space.)

19 PLACE OF BURIAL, CREMATION OR REMOVAL Portland Ore
DATE OF BURIAL Nov 5 1927
20 UNDERTAKER Marion Veatch
ADDRESS Eugene

Henry Jackson Day's Death certificate. His death is marked from "Acute Cardiac Dialation," November 4, 1927. *Jan and Mike.*

Withers had just bought property himself and did not have the funds available at the time the embezzlement was revealed. He went to the bank and obtained a personal loan, which he paid back out of his salary as he earned it. I never heard how it came to be that Day came back to Lane County/Oregon and appeared to live a normal life thereafter.

However, if the funds had been replaced by Withers and no charges were ever filed against Day, there was effectively no crime, except in the public eye. It also appears that Henry Jackson Day and his first wife divorced between 1900 and 1910, which would have been a scandal of its own at the time in history.[82]

Did Henry Jackson Day live off the stolen money for the whole time he was gone? It wasn't a small sum: $2,110.49 in 1899 dollars is $76,114.05 in 2024. Even if it was a large amount, living on that sum for thirty years seems unlikely. Or did he work his way around the country until he thought the coast was clear? The only indications of any ill will to Day by anyone are his divorce, his theft and his daughter's snub by not naming him in her obituary. Granted, those are big things to hurdle. We can only wonder what Henry Jackson did in those lost years, and more, what his relatives thought when he finally came back.

7

THE LONG PURSUIT OF BERT HEATON

On March 19, 1901, Bert a.k.a. "Ray" Heaton walked into the bar at the Monogram Saloon not long after midnight with one goal: to rob the place. He made his way inside with stealth and shot the bartender without anyone seeing who he was. Heaton committed the cold, brutal murder of bartender Benton Tracy, apparently unseen, in the dead of night. After the murder, he rifled through the till and "secured about $300.00," according to *The Plaindealer* newspaper,[83] or almost $3,700 today.

> *No one saw the deed, but Bert Heaton, known there as Ray, a gambler, was strongly suspected of the crime, and he left Junction that night. He is about 28 years old. At the coroner's inquest, Heaton was accused of the murder, and the grand jury brought in an indictment against him of murder in the first degree. The evidence against Heaton, while circumstantial, is strong enough to convict, it is said.*[84]

There really seemed to be no motive for the murder except for the money. When investigators researched Bert Heaton, he was thought by many to be a degenerate gambler by profession. He had traveled north to Oregon to gamble after the "games were shut down" in his previous home of Redding, California. Heaton's gambling was at a point where he was down on his luck, and he was in a pattern of losing and owing money. Most articles about the murder had a deep undertone condemning the vice that gambling was seen to be.

Clement Hode's Saloon and Billiard Hall, in 1892. Directory located on the west side of Willamette Street, on the northwest corner of the alley between Eighth and Ninth Avenues. Interior. View shows bar and three unidentified men, including the bartender. *Lane County History Museum.*

Sheriff Withers was called for, and when he arrived, Heaton had disappeared. There was no news of Heaton for over two months. Withers traced his quarry's background and traveled across several states and a large swath of the west to get his man, as the newspapers blasted out:

> *The Sheriff was unable to get any clue to his whereabouts until June 24 (1902) when he heard of him in Redding. He at once went in pursuit, but the man was gone. Keeping up the search he located him in Wells, Nevada, where he made his arrest in a barber shop, and now has his prisoner behind bars.*[85]

A comprehensive article in the *Corvallis Times* stated the evidence shown at Heaton's trial for Benton Tracy's death.

> *That at about 12:15 on the night of May 19th six shots were fired, the first shot sounded as distant, and that within a minute five shots followed in quick succession; that Burt Heaton was a gambler "broke;" that 50 cents was given him that night which he lost in a game; that sundry persons had given him money at about that time to buy meals; that he was seen in the stairway 10 feet N*[orth] *of the center of the front door of the Monogram*

THE WHEEL THAT CAN'T BE STOPPED;—IT'S HUMAN NATURE.

"The wheel that can't be stopped;—it's human nature." A large red devil turns the crank of a large wheel decorated with scenes labeled "Reformers," "Citizen's Committee," "Women's League" and "Salvation," as well as police officers hanging onto the wheel as it spins, 1901. *S.D. Erhart, Library of Congress, Prints & Photographs Division, Washington, D.C.*

> *at 11 pm on the night of the murder; that he was seen by two persons in front of the saloon within five minutes of the shooting…All these parties identified the murderer as Burt Ray—the deft Heaton.*[86]

The article also mentioned a more thorough accounting of what the killer had stolen from the till. It was less than originally estimated. He got away with five or six dollars in dimes, a dollar in nickels and eight or nine twenty-dollar gold pieces in a buckskin leather pouch. Someone who resembled Heaton was spotted leaving town at one o'clock in the morning. He was next seen at a boardinghouse at 8:30 a.m.. He stated that he was fatigued and "stayed in his room until supper," at which he inquired about the train station. The wife of the couple who ran the boardinghouse positively identified Heaton.

The next sighting of Heaton, in Redding, was after a long train ride where he had said he "came through as blind baggage and beat the railroad company." There he met a man to whom he owed a dollar. He bragged to this man that he had enough money to get to Sacramento and then Arizona. He told that man that he had traveled long, arrived late and stayed at the Martins' boardinghouse in Redding, where he ravenously ate an enormous breakfast as he "had not eaten for two days." Heaton was met at the Martins by "Slivers," who was his girlfriend masquerading as his wife. He took Slivers shopping after breakfast and bought her several things, including a small purse. They said that Benton's time in Oregon had been rough, but that they "got the stuff" as a result and that "Betsey [referring to his revolver] had served him well." Mrs. Martins, the boardinghouse owner, picked Slivers's purse up to remark on it; she dropped two gold five- and ten-dollar pieces, as well as several other silver coins.

Heaton and Slivers traveled onward by train, eventually landing in Wells, Nevada. Sheriff Withers traced him there, and Heaton was arrested on July 19, 1902, at a barbershop in Wells. Mrs. Martins, the chief of police in Redding and the sheriff of Redding all affirmed that they were familiar with the revolver that was found on Heaton and used to kill Tracy. The Redding Police Department had been in custody of said gun earlier in 1902. It was first referred to there as "Old Betsey."

Benton did not testify in his own defense. Bert Heaton's wife/girlfriend Slivers was brought to Eugene for the trial of her husband. She stated firmly that she knew that "he was innocent."[87] The jury didn't have to deliberate for long. In just two hours, they returned with a guilty verdict and he was sentenced to life in prison.

Benton Tracy was remembered as a respected and honorable kind of man. The bartender was first trained as a blacksmith in Albany, Oregon, and worked there and later in Corvallis after his first wife died. He and his second wife, a schoolteacher, lived in various places around the Willamette Valley, and he worked at the Monogram Saloon for a few years prior to the time of his murder. The community mourned him deeply, and the last article written about his death said, "That his miserable murderer should escape the rope is most deeply regretted."[88]

The doctor who conducted his autopsy mentioned that his death was likely a quick one. He said of Tracy:

> *He was a man that attended to his own business. He never interfered with anyone else....He was leaning on the bar facing the front; facing the mirror and down on the drain board with his back to the north. Just looked as peaceful and quiet as if he had gone to sleep.*[89]

8

IT'S A DANGEROUS BUSINESS, WALKING OUT YOUR DOOR

Freak Accidents and Horrible Ways to Die

The sheer brutality of the majority of the deaths contained in the Lane County coroner's reports is a shock. Not only the brutality, but also the accidental nature of so many of them, and the possibility that several of them could have been prevented with the technology available today, takes one's breath away. All the reports in this chapter are stark reminders of the dangers that lurked everywhere in the late 1800s–early 1900s Eugene area.

These reports were often no more than a sheet or two of paper. It underscored the tragic nature of the box of coroner's reports in a whole different way. One such case was that of Hattie Sumner. The report, one page alone, was about "a child found dead." There are no photos in the archives and no other information. It's a brief, sad story in just a few sentences.

> *We, the jury, find as follows:*
> *1st. The name of the deceased is Hattie Sumner.*
> *2nd. That the deceased is Seven years past.*
> *3rd. That the deceased was a white female person of American Birth.*
> *4th. That she died on the 16th day of April 1908, in Eugene, Lane County, Oregon, and that the cause of her death was by being run over by a streetcar at the corner of Thirteenth and Alder Streets and that if the Mother had used proper caution the accident might not have happened.*[90]

"Streetcars—Testing Devices for Saving Lives on Car Fenders." This is an example of inventions to prevent injury by streetcars, similar to "cattle catchers" mounted on trains. 1908. *George Grantham Bain Collection, Library of Congress.*

"Back in the 1920s, most American city-dwellers took public transportation to work every day," reported Joseph Stromberg for *Vox*, but he added, "What really killed the streetcar: gridlock and artificially low fares."[91] The streetcars and their resultant deaths became mostly obsolete as other modes of transport used the same roads. The advent of the cheap and available

Model T created different accident opportunities. Streetcars "could travel as fast as twenty miles per hour, " much faster than the old-fashioned, quaint downtown-touring usages of today suggest, but nowhere near as fast as a car could go.[92]

Trains were something to worry about as well. In August 1909, John Michaels, age fifty-nine; Ray Swartz, age eighteen, and George Bailey, age seventeen, were all in a train when they died. Southern Pacific Passenger train no. 17 wrecked when it struck a bull that belonged to Nancy Bushnell. "They came by their death as a result of the wreck," and the train was "on their back about 9:20 p.m., one and one-half miles south of Eugene." The wreck was "unavoidable," and the coroner ruled "that no blame is attached to anybody."[93]

Earlier that year, a twenty-year-old had lost his life to a train in an accident. The coroner "believed by the jury from evidence given, [the victim] to have been Fred W. Johnson."

> [We the jury find] *That he died on the 4th day of April, 1908, in Eugene, Lane County, Oregon, and the cause of his death was accidental and due to his own acts. That he was the victim of an accident which occurred in the depot yard of the Southern Pacific RR Company, in Eugene. That the deceased attempted to board a moving freight train, and, missing his hold, was thrown in such a manner that his feet were severed by the wheels and his skull crushed by contact with some part of the car trucks. That death was principally due to the injury on the head and was almost instantaneous.*

Mercifully, the report closed by saying that "death was due principally to the injury on the head and was almost instantaneous."[94]

Another difficult-to-read coroner's report was accompanied by a still-bright-yellow telegram in its file. The story it told was almost too awful to describe, so I will quote it here:

> *Coroner Harris,*
> *Eugene, Oregon, March 29, 1888*
>
> *Lee Mount, a boy killed by freight train at Saginaw. Body torn all to pieces. Shall we gather the remains and bring here.*
>
> *James Heminway.*

The report itself explained that "Leland Mount, 17 years of age and an assistant of Lemati [a railroad station], came to his death by attempting to board a moving freight train, and falling on the track was run over by cars."[95]

The many ways to die doing everyday activities included some bizarre deaths while at work. Chester W. Jessie, twenty years old, died in a particularly awful way.

> *He and J.A. McCauley had been removing clay from a pit at the Eugene Brick Yard (3 miles West). They had undermined a portion of the bank to bring down the clay, or rather loosen it up.*

From roughly the middle of the 1800s to the early 1900s, the process of making bricks included digging out clay, often from marshy areas. As much of the Willamette Valley and Eugene is marshy, there were many places to dig up materials around town. After raw clay was dug, it was mixed together with crushed shells, shale or sand. This slurry was packed into molds in earlier times. By the early 1900s, the mixture was packed into a brickmaking machine invented in 1863 that extruded the material in a thick ribbon before being cut, stacked and dried. The raw material still needed to be gathered before that, however, and at the time, the most efficient way was to simply dig it out.[96] Jessie's coroner's report tells what happened in stark detail:

> *The earth dropped where they were not expecting it, catching Mr. Jessie under it. His life was crushed out instantly. They had not been careful enough. The foreman had spoken to them just prior to the accident not to take too many chances.*[97]

Occasionally, death was recorded as simply a desperate attempt at greed, for purposes unknown. On August 5, 1906, seventy-year-old William Powell died of a gunshot wound. In an interesting addition to his file, a very clear version of what happened to Powell came from the attending physician Dr. William F. Best, even if it was secondhand:

> *Dr. Hockett sent for me to come and see the deceased Sunday evening and I went to the depot where he was. I examined the (man who is now) deceased and found a bullet wound on the left side which had pierced the tenth rib and fractured it....I probed the wound and discovered some of the contents of the stomach. I told him that his hours were numbered.*

Pettit's brickyard. Photograph shows men with horses with carts near a pit in the ground, where men dug for clay under a wooden frame structure. 1900. *Jacob Riis, Library of Congress, Prints & Photographs Division, Washington, D.C.*

Dr. Best continued with the information he had learned about the patient's life:

> *We brought him to Dr. Hockett's office and made him as comfortable as possible. He saw my Grand Army button and told me that he was a Union Soldier and had served in the army of the Potomac in the 122nd regiment of the Pennsylvania Infantry. That he had served four years and one-half and had been dishonorably discharged for striking a superior officer. That he had gone through the battle of Gettysburg without a scratch and to be now shot down by a couple of hoodlums was too bad.*

Powell had been camping near the Willamette River when he was assaulted:

> *He said there was two boys came along. He had some provisions. They wanted to take it from him. He told them that he would not give it up and to go away. The smaller one of the two says: "Damn you, I'll fix you." And then he shot me. The man died at 25 minutes to 8 o'clock this morning. We held a post mortem exam under the direction of the coroner and traced the course of the bullet. We found it on the right side of the thyroid vertebrae of the lumbar region.*[98]

Fred Bailey, twenty-nine, was quoted in the report as having found Powell near the railroad bridge. He initially thought the older man's leg was broken but found the bullet hole and brought him to Dr. Hockett. "The old man told me he was cooking supper," Bailey said, "And 'I got some meat done and the boys wanted to eat it and I asked them to go away and let me alone' and one of them shot him."

Bailey was able to deduce that he had also seen the boys around 5:00 or 5:30 that night.

> *When the train came along the brakeman told me he had put two boys off the train and the larger of the two had pulled a revolver on him. He asked me to arrest him. I asked him if he would prosecute the boy and he said no, but to arrest him anyway.*

The boys were brought in, and Bailey asked them if they had a revolver. The older replied that he had a .38 Smith and Wesson pearl handle in a holster at his belt. Bailey, under the idea that it was not truly illegal to carry a revolver, told them that they could go but they were not wanted in town. He gave them a little time to get something to eat, and then they turned toward the river. This was apparently when they shot Powell. The smaller boy was named Hugh Saxon, fourteen, and the larger boy, approximately eighteen to twenty, was Tommy Reaves. Both worked in the ironworks in Portland. Tommy Reaves told Bailey that "he wanted to go the northern route back to Chicago but that the kid wanted to go this way, and he said he was going to please the kid."

Butcher Fred Bartels, twenty-nine, concurred with the story told by the others. He had sat up with Powell after he was taken to the doctor. His testimony shed a little more light on William Powell's life:

> *He told me…that he had three boys and they were of no account. He said he had a daughter working in a corset factory in Frisco. Said he had*

> *a brother running a shoe shop in Seattle. He said his brother's name was Frederick Powell. He was perfectly conscious during the time that he was talking to me. He told me that he thought he was going to die.*[99]

Despite all this testimony, the boys were not found or prosecuted for the crime because William Powell's coroner's report found that his death was "from a person or persons unknown." It is a sad entry and a look into the kind of desperation that might have driven a person to commit such a terrible act on a person just sitting down to eat his dinner. It used to be commonplace for families to have a dozen children, and not only for a labor force on the farms. In late nineteenth-century America, "nearly one out of every five children died before the age of five."[100] Oregon, and Eugene itself, weren't exempt from this statistic.

Take the case of Raymond Oliver Miller. Even a pleasant outing could lead to tragedy. F.A. Miller, father of two and farm caretaker, was with his children on the evening of November 9, 1900. They'd asked him to play with them and go out to their field together:

> *Little Raymond wanted his papa to roll a log down hill to see it roll. Mr. Miller, in order to amuse him, got a good sized log in place all ready to roll; the little fellow was to start it. In some way or other his clothes were caught upon the log, which threw him over it and directly in its path. In a flash, before even the horrified father could speak, the log had passed, leaving behind the crushed remains of the little boy. Death was almost instantaneous.*[101]

The lives of both children and adults were difficult at best and often tragic. Notices of deaths from what are now largely preventable illnesses were in the newspapers and coroners' reports daily.

> *Died—At the home of his parents, Mr. and Mrs S. Fawver, near this city, Thursday evening, February 6, 1908, Howard Fawver, aged six months and two days, of membranous croup. He was a bright little child, and his death was a sad blow to his parents and their many friends.*[102]

Even in cases that did not result in death, circumstances made things harder and life more poignant. It's astounding to a modern eye to read an advertisement for adoption in the same article as news about the desertion of a baby:

Mother Deserts Three-Month-Old Babe

Mrs. Geo. H. Kelly, of the local juvenile court, has another child—a wee babe—on hand which can be had for adoption by some responsible person. The child, a girl three months old, was brought to her before breakfast by its grandfather, W.J. Peyburn, who stated that its mother, Mrs. Charles Edwards had deserted it and left it with its grandparents. They were unable to care for it and turned it over to Mrs. Kelly. Mr. Peyburn states that the baby's father deserted his wife some time before the baby was born, and that the mother left only a few days ago, saying that she would have nothing more to do with the child.[103]

9

THE SIREN SONG OF THE CALLIOPE

John Seymour

In 1903, the idea of a circus coming to town was a banner day that was looked forward to for months. Indeed, "The arrival of the circus in a small town was among the most exciting events in the lives of rural Americans," according to Mina Elwell in an article titled "What 19th Century Circus Life Was Really Like."

She went on to explain how the experience of seeing the well-trained performers, exotic acts and wild animals was often "a one-in-a-lifetime experience" for many.[104] This was likely even more true in a semirural area, as Eugene was at the time.

Those who worked at the circus were there for various reasons. The jobs were regular, whether as a performer or staff; the food was plentiful; and a residence, however itinerant, was provided. Children who were orphans or runaways joined up to learn a trade and were prized as cheap labor. Those who grew up in the business tended to stay there.

It's no surprise, then, that John Seymour, a twenty-two-year-old circus man previously incarcerated in the penitentiary in Salem, was spotted in the Ringling Brothers Circus in Eugene in 1903. He could not stay away.

Seymour had been first jailed on November 14, 1902, for larceny and received a sentence of eighteen months. He had broken into the Reliable Loan Office and stolen items like guns and valuables. Eight months into that sentence, or around the first week of August 1903, he was made a "trusty." A trusty was an inmate who had proven their worth and was trusted to do jobs or go out to work outside prison walls and then come back for dinner. They resided inside the prison at night.

Circus Day in Oregon, 1943. An example of what the entrance to the circus was like in a small town. *Russell Lee, photographer, Library of Congress.*

For the first three weeks of his relative freedom, he was employed as a waiter in the prison's employee dining room. The dining hall where he worked was in the front of the prison's main building. It was still behind the iron gates of the penitentiary proper, but the trusties were allowed to go back and forth to the outside to do chores like the retrieval of supplies and firewood.

On Wednesday, August 27, 1903, Seymour and the other trusties left their cells when released for work at five o'clock in the morning. Instead of proceeding to his job, Seymour went directly to the prison stables and took his leave from there largely unnoticed. When they found he was gone, authorities searched the grounds but did not find him.

> *Seymour was an old circus employee, and ever since hearing the Ringling Brothers' circus was coming he has shown considerable interest in the event, talking about it a great deal. Possibly he wanted to see the performance, but more likely a hankering for the old busy life around the great shows took possession of him, and he decided to escape and make an attempt to join them and leave the country. If so, the state will be well rid of him.*[105]

Though he was said to have wanted to join the circus badly, the newspapers said it was unlikely. A reward was set at $50.00 ($1,870.09 in 2024). Prison officials launched a search immediately. In short order, the prison superintendent had posters printed that gave Seymour's description:

> *Small build. Cut scar point chin. Cut scar back of right wrist. India ink mark blue, representing letters "C.B.," below is five-point star inside of lower right arm. India ink mark blue, representing circle "O," right hand between at base of thumb and index finger. Brown stain, right hip. Large vaccine mark outside left upper arm. Pit scar inside right knee. Teeth good...Height 5 feet 3½ inches. Weight 132 pounds. Complexion light. Black hair. Eyes blue.*[106]

Authorities found that a stablemaster near the prison had been away from his post on the morning when Seymour escaped. Ironically, the man, Robert Wiggins, was off to see the circus be built. A bay horse with a black mane was stolen sometime when he was gone, between five and six o'clock in the morning. The authorities assumed when they heard this news that Seymour was long gone from the area by the time the theft was discovered.

The next stop for Ringling Brothers was Albany, Oregon, and then Eugene. Ringling Brothers Circus detectives, who apparently were staple employees there, were put on the lookout for the convict and were quoted as saying: "I will do all in my power to assist in capturing the convict, and he cannot join my shows, as I don't want that kind of man."

They may not have wanted him, but they apparently got him. A newspaper on August 28, the day after he ran, mentions Seymour joining the circus train in Eugene. The circus in Eugene came into town on "87 double-length train cars, all heavily loaded with wild animals, tents, and performers."[107] The load-out area took up over fifteen acres of space; to put the size in context, one acre is roughly the size of an American football field, so the space it took up to load-in was about the equivalent size of fifteen football fields. The largest tent boasted the ability to hold eighteen thousand people.

In the main tent, the first part of the Ringling Brothers show was a 1,200-person performance of *Jerusalem and the Crusades*. This main event was often called the "spec," or spectacle procession of as many performers as they could fit in. It included a ballet with "extravagant costumes." Next was the performance of three different elephant troupes. After that came a display of sixty-one trained horses and then two groups of trained seals performed. Next came a hallmark of the circus, the large, terrifying performance by acrobats and aerialists where they soared at huge heights over flimsy nets. When it was done, the performers got ready to do the whole performance again. At the same time as the main acts, smaller acts ran concurrently, most notably the *Oddities Show* of performers with sideshow acts. After the last big

Circus Day in Oregon. 1942. *Russell Lee, photographer, Library of Congress.*

show, it took a very short time—less than an hour, in one account—to take it all down and load up for the next city.[108]

The reports from the Eugene circus praised the calliope as "the wonder of the parade." They extolled one particular act, saying, "One of the sideshows contained a man with three legs, all in use." The circus strained the sleeping and dining capacities of the city of 24,658. The newspaper also noted,

> *The elephants were watered this morning on south Willamette Street. The big beasts drank barrels of water supplied by the city.... The clowns were the funniest ever seen.*[109]

Seymour was supposed to have made it to Eugene and caught up with the circus there. Though the officers kept an eye out for the convict, he was not found. Little wonder that, in light of the number of people employed by the circus. He had been heard to speak of friends in the profession while he was talking about the circus before he escaped from prison. And with the first name John, it was probably not all that hard for him to join up under a false last name. Reports differ on where he was seen exactly, but it seems likely that joining up with the circus again, which he wanted to do so much he escaped prison, was exactly what he did. He was rumored to have been a "Canvas Man," someone strong who helped carry and put up the tents. The circus spent several days in Eugene. It was possibly a good place to harvest an audience from smaller cities nearby. The newspapers noted that smaller towns were virtual ghost towns when the circus was around. Almost everyone was there, plus people from any neighboring place who could get there. A few papers said that drunks and fights were notably absent due to the entire populations being inside the circus proper.

The next report of John Seymour wasn't until September 4, 1903. The circus spent winters in Bridgeport, Connecticut, and he wasn't bound for that state. Seymour instead had taken the train to Portland, where he committed a crime. Unbelievably, he broke into the same building he had broken into the first time he went to prison, the Reliable Loan Office, where he retrieved more guns and musical instruments. He remained on the run until he reached Tacoma, Washington, where he was once again caught and returned to jail.

Upon his completion of the original sentence plus additional time, he was released.[110] In a stunning turn of events, Seymour was swiftly rearrested, this time for a charge of burglary in Washington, D.C. His captor, U.S. Marshal J.A. Wilson, who lived in Oregon, happened to be getting married to Elizabeth Gore. The Wilsons married immediately and "left on an eastern bridal trip accompanied by John Seymour alias Barton, wanted at Washington D.C. for burglary, and U.S. Marshal Mathews, all going to Washington."[111] Seymour was also formerly known as George Martin.

The police department stated, "His presence will in no way mar the pleasure of the trip of the bride and groom."[112]

Seymour was remanded in Washington, D.C., on schedule and showed no remorse for his crimes During his trial, he was nonplussed and seemingly uncaring about his crimes.

> *The accused man was as cool as the proverbial cucumber…and appeared to have no concern of what became of him. He talked freely about his crimes, admitting them unblushingly—even with an apparent satisfaction.*

The authorities and public were appalled at Seymour's attitude, particularly that he didn't apologize or seem sorry for the things that he had done.

> *When asked if he did not feel some compunctions of conscience about the crimes he committed, he replied: "No, why should I? I don't feel that I have done anything wrong when I rob a man who has more than I have. I can enjoy myself on money that I have stolen just as well as if I had earned it honestly. Why shouldn't I?"*[113]

Seymour went on trial and went back to jail in Washington, D.C. His name leaves the public record after that point. He is remembered as a criminal, yes, but one with a curious penchant and longing to return to circus life in little Eugene, Oregon.

Old Capital Prison, Washington, D.C., circa 1860–65. John Seymore's home after his final arrest. *Mathew Benjamin Brady, U.S. National Archives and Records Administration.*

10
PREJUDICE RAMPANT

The Dark Violence of Inherent Racism in Eugene

Some of the opaque parts of the coroner's reports related to women or to people who were nonwhite. Racism is a thorny issue for those studying Oregon history because the state was literally set up as a racist utopia. "Oregon's constitution was not uncommon, as a state in the Union still struggling with the post-Civil War racial divide, in having exclusionary articles written into it."[114] One such exclusionary article read:

> *Article I Section 35—No free Negro, or Mulatto, not residing in this State at the time of the adoption of this Constitution, shall come, reside, or be in this State, or hold any real estate, or make any contracts, or maintain any suit therein; and the Legislative Assembly shall provide by penal laws for the removal, by public officers, of all such negroes, and mulattoes, and for their effectual exclusion from the State, and for the punishment of persons who shall bring them into the State, or employ, or harbor them.*[115]

The people who migrated to Oregon during the Manifest Destiny period were predominantly white. America's Great Migration Project, funded by the University of Washington, states in its report that when Oregon became a state on Valentine's Day 1859, the population was mostly made up of whites from mainly the Midwest region of the United States. However, in 1900, that website also counted 9,728 Oregon residents who were from China and 2,110 who were from Japan. These people built strong communities in large cities like Vancouver, San Francisco and Portland to begin with and smaller

Members of the Eugene Mining Company pose in front of a mining building at an unidentified site north of Blue River, 1890. *Lane County History Museum.*

groups where the immigrants could find work. Much of that work was in manual labor (mining, logging, railroad work) so wasn't seen as consequential by the societies they built. Many still have vibrant communities today.[116]

Consequent to their erasure from newspaper and public information, very few of the reports were written about anyone who was not white or male. One of the reports was one page, written on April 30, 1900. The report was written on paper that had been printed the previous century; the "189..." was crossed out to write the correct year. The county coroner at the time, Waldo L. Cheshire, MD, wrote:

> *Sir,*
>
> *Enclosed please note the findings of the coroner's inquest in the case of a Japanese who having suddenly died in camp at the Mohawk Bridge, on the night of April 27 1900. Suspecting, from the recent importation of so many Japanese, a case of the "Bubonic Plague," I made a thorough external examination. But not finding sufficient evidence as to the condition of the body and from witnesses I did not go to the expense of a post-mortem examination.*
>
> *Yours respectfully, W.L. Cheshire, Coroner*

The coroner's suspicion of bubonic plague specifically wasn't (only) a racist supposition of the "other." There had truly been an outbreak of bubonic plague in San Francisco in 1900, and there was even an article about said outbreak in the June 2, 1900 issue of *Harper's Weekly*, so the news of the outbreak may have been rumored or even seen farther north. The California community where the outbreak happened was Chinese, not Japanese, but the small-town Oregon doctor evidently did not care to differentiate. A large number of Chinese and Japanese immigrants moved to the West Coast of the United States during the latter half of the 1800s for various reasons, including mining, railroad work or simply for a better life.

People confined within the Chinese quarter, cooking their meals. "The Bubonic Plague in San Francisco," *Harper's Weekly*, 1900. *Cabinet of American Illustration, Library of Congress.*

Sadly, the casual treatment of Coroner Cheshire in this case was nothing out of the ordinary. In July 1891, Acting Coroner J.S. Mealy Jr. wrote a report of Native woman Julia Fisherman's death, with the results of the inquisition being a litany of her alcoholism and an undetermined cause, despite suspicious circumstances. Drawings and engravings of Native people of the time were mainly stereotypical, as in this drawing that uses the "Indian Maiden," stereotype, beautiful though it may be.

Whether the doubtful conclusion of Fisherman's report was purposefully opaque isn't known, but the physical examination certainly seems cursory. The first to be interviewed was noted as "Sally Fisherman (Indian)." Her testimony raises some questions

> *Julia Fisherman, whose body is being held, is my step-mother. I saw Julia Tuesday evening and she was not sick. I was sleeping in the tent. Julia did not go to bed that night thought I know I saw her in the house. After I went to bed I saw a man outside at the road. I heard him whistle, it was Hugh Bowman. Did not see him have any whisky. Julia went out to where Bowman was, remained about 20 minutes. The last I saw of Julia, she*

> *came back to the house.* [I] *Did not see Bowman any more. Bowman did not talk to me. I do not know what they were talking about. The first I saw of Boren was after I went to bed.*[117]

The next to testify was "Enouch Bob (Indian)." His story didn't bring much clarity to the situation.

> *I am acquainted with Julia Fisherman, over whose body this inquisition is now pending. I found out she died about 1 o'clock Wednesday morning. I went home from town about 10 o'clock Tuesday night and saw Julia in the house- they had not gone to bed. I went to bed directly after going home. Met Hugh Bowman on the Rail Road track as I went home near the Rail Road bridge. Julia was a little sick when I got home.*[118]

"Mary Bob (Indian)" was sworn in after that. Her testimony helped some but raised a mystery as well:

> *Her name is Julia Fishman. I helped Julia wash the day before she died. I went home—Julia went home about 7 o'clock. She did not say anything about sick. Did not see her go to bed. Did not see Mr. Bowman. Heard him whistle, Julia told me it was Hugh Bowman after he came back—and that she was afraid. Bowman wanted to take her to Bohemia. Julia said Bowman had a bottle. She thought it was medicine. Saw her at nine o'clock in the evening and did not see her again until the next morning at 6 o'clock when we found her dead.*[119]

The last of the citizens to testify before the coroner's jury was Polk Scott. He said that he "left town a little after sundown." When he went to the train depot, he saw Hugh Bowman, who told him to let Julia know that "he wanted her to go to Bohemia with him," and that "he had a good horse for her to ride, and that he wanted her to go that night." Bowman told Scott that he would rejoin Julia at the Bohemia Camp later that night. Bowen even gave Scott $0.10 (about $3.75 in 2024 dollars) to give Julia the message to meet him there.

At the Fishman house, Scott heard someone whistle in the evening. Julia went outside. When she came back, she said Mr. Bowen was outside. Polk did not know where she died but thought she'd died where she had been found. He affirmed that he had no whiskey that night, though he had lied to the sheriff and told him he was drunk because he was mad. Polk was also quick to assure the jury that Bowman did not come inside the house and that Julia went out once—but she may have gone out again after he went to sleep.

The last page of the coroner's report includes his final statement. Acting Coroner J.S. Mealy concluded that after "an external examination of the body, and found no traces of violence." He concluded that "the deceased died from natural causes," despite "marks on her neck." He instead thought the "marks on the neck were caused by some article of clothing coming in contact with the skin which colored the same."

It's a vague wording but sounds an awful lot like she might have died by strangulation. The curious phrase of death being "contact caused by some article of clothing" sets off warning bells, but the official pronouncement was that there was "no indication of apoplexy." Mealy said that instead, he would "infer that death was caused from heart failure superseded by intoxication."[120]

11
MAYHEM AT ISHAM'S CORRAL

The word trickled into Eugene, as the home-to-home gossip pipeline often shared news in 1898, and finally it became widely known: John Linn, a sixty-year-old stockman, had been killed by his young trail companion. Claude Branton murdered Linn as he lay around the campfire where they had stopped for the night, in a place called Isham's Corral, en route to the valley.

Rumors flew. It was hard to understand why Branton, about forty-five years old and who had not been otherwise known as a violent or murderous man, would have done such a thing. He, his friend John Linn and Courtland Green had been driving a group of horses over the mountains to Eugene. They "had trouble over a settlement at Squaw Creek, Crook County,"[121] but had reached their stop-off destination at Alder Creek, outside Eugene, to stay the night on June 15, 1898. The horses had been corralled for the night. Linn was stretched out on his back next to the fire at about ten o'clock when Green, who had his arms full of wood, heard the report of a gun.

When Green looked back, he saw Branton standing over Linn with a smoking pistol in his hand. Linn had been shot in the head. According to Green's initial statement, he did not know what happened to the body of John Linn after he was murdered. When he and Branton drove the horses on to Walterville the next day, to be distributed throughout the Willamette Valley, Green confessed what he had seen to his uncle, who lived there, and that he didn't interfere because he was afraid Branton would kill him too. Green's uncle then made him ride for Eugene to tell the local law enforcement and telegraphed Sheriff W.W. Withers. What Green confessed to that day was not the whole story, however.

The story became muddied after the lawmen started to inquire about the residents who lived near the murder site and along the path the two took down the river.

> *Conversation with people along the river develops that Branton offered Walter Millican and Lawrence Millican either money or horses to swear that they bought horses from Linn on this side of the mountains or at Walterville. He also offered money or horses to the following men to say that they had bought horses from Linn in the Valley or talked with him about them: Walden Trotter, Walter Trotter, David Fountain, Jas Allen, Zera Potter and Anson Potter.*[122]

The search for Branton continued up and down the valley. It was found that after arriving in Walterville, Branton had disguised his identity as that of Linn to safely pasture the horses with a man named William Seavey. Word arrived that after that, Linn/Branton had bought a bicycle and a new set of clothing with money that he had previously sent to his friend and his and Green's former employer, a Mr. Smeed, for safekeeping. Smeed said to authorities that "Green worked for him several years and he considered the boy trustworthy in every respect."

In light of Branton's subterfuge about his identity, more accurate photographs and drawings were circulated through all known areas that the pair had congregated. They also offered a $250 reward for the man's arrest and conviction.[123] He was recorded as having visited his uncle in Pleasant Hill but afterward seemed to have disappeared into thin air. While the authorities were looking for Branton, they placed Courtland Green under arrest as an accessory in Eugene with a $7,500 bond, which he did not pay and remained in jail.[124]

Sightings of Branton were reported sporadically in various places. The most concrete clues were a quote from Linn that he wanted to join the army and a sighting of him "waiting for the south-bound overland California Express at Creswell, Lane County, Or., Sunday night, July 3, 1898."[125] It was assumed that Branton had joined the army, perhaps under an assumed name, and was gone; still, the authorities kept up the search for him.

Meanwhile, at the site of Linn's murder, the searchers found a large burned log in the clearing where they'd camped. The log was more a felled tree trunk and was half charred on one side where it lay on the ground. "The campfire had been built against one side of a soaked, rotten log, and between two tall fir trees, one about two feet in diameter and one about 18 inches," the report said. "The fire was one of the cleanest I ever saw. No burnt sticks were left around the edge, but all were burned clean, and it was evident that Branton watched the fire all night, pushing the embers into the center of the fire until everything had been consumed."[126]

They also found scraps of clothing and a few burned bones. After the coroner and inspectors visited the site, they said:

> *The body had been cremated in the camp-fire and so carefully had the fiendish butcher accomplished his horrible task all that could be recovered by the officers was a few charred bones, buttons and suspender buckles etc. A section of the skull, a portion of the lower jaw, toe joint and some teeth are all that can be positively identified as having belonged to a human body. The suspender buckles found are of rather large size and bear the word "GLADIATOR," on middle bar.*[127]

The crime became more macabre the longer they looked at the scene. More details clarified that any remains they found were those of John Linn. It also became obvious that much more had happened in that clearing than a simple case of murder. The coroner found that

> *an axe, found beside the campfire stained with blood, had evidently been used by the murderer to chop the body of his victim into small pieces to facilitate the work of cremation. Taken altogether it was one of the most cold-blooded and atrocious crimes ever committed in the state.*[128]

John Linn was a well-known and highly regarded Oregon resident, having been in the farming and stockwork industry for about twelve or thirteen years before he died. He had saved up quite a bit of money due to his hard work and good business dealings, had worked on other people's farms and owned the herd of horses they were driving across the mountains to find a better place for them to pasture long-term. He rented a room from a farming family for many years and was a member of the Woodsmen of the World fraternal organization.

Claude Branton and his mother lived in the eastern side of the valley for the winters. Mrs. Branton had gotten a divorce from her husband in April 1898. The rumor mill said that John Linn was romantically interested in

A close-up view of site of murder site of John A. Linn by Claude Branton at Isham's Corral, 1898. Linn was lying with his head against tree in background right, with burned bark on its left side, when he was shot. *Dr. Waldo Cheshire, Lane County History Museum.*

Mrs. Branton and even that some time before the horse drive, the two had run off to Washington to get married. That fact was unsubstantiated but interesting nonetheless. It was particularly so since Linn had that substantial nest egg, a $3,000 life insurance policy with the Woodsmen of the World and "no known relatives on this coast," according to *The Globe.*

The coroner removed the remains of Linn to his office for trial. The coroner's jury and report officially accused Claude Branton of John Linn's murder for reasons unknown. Officers, including Deputy Sheriff Henry Day, traveled to San Francisco to find Branton. A description went out through multiple states to aid them in case he was recognized:

> *Claude Branton, age about 21; height, about 5 ft 8 in.; weight 180 pounds; black, coarse hair; eyes dark; even, white teeth; smooth shaved; wore dark suit, frock coat, black Fedora hat; wore no. 8 shoe; square built; full chested;*

> *smiles and laughs while talking. Will probably tell about bringing drove of horses from eastern Oregon to Willamette Valley.*[129]

It seemed like the posters and description worked. A few days later, he was seen north in The Dalles, Canyon Creek, Canyon City, and further:

> *E.L. Robbins…said that the supposed murderer was seen by different persons…who had ample opportunity to converse with him and thoroughly scrutinize him. He said that there was no doubt that it was Branton. He was driving a horse attached to a cart and was making very fast time when on the road away from the more thickly settled parts. Some time after his departure from Canyon City, officers started in pursuit and traced him for twenty miles to the Allen store in Fox Valley, six miles south of Long Creek. It was ascertained there that the fugitive had been seen at that place Monday morning. Nothing more has been seen or heard of him since, although the entire country, which is thickly settled, has been scoured by searchers.*[130]

Claude Branton was caught after he departed the train at the Eugene station and walked down the street on July 21, 1898. He arrived in the afternoon and was walking down Willamette Street in downtown Eugene when a man named Al Auten, a "well-known cigar dealer," recognized him and went for the sheriff. Sheriff Henry Day immediately went looking on the streets, found Branton and arrested him, all within moments of being told he had been spotted. Branton admitted no guilt and told the sheriff that at Pleasant Hill at the end of July, he went to Topeka, Kansas, to find some work. Having found no work, he said he was only returning home.[131] By 2:30 p.m. on July 21, he was in jail.

In a surprising turn, the city of Eugene Deputy District Attorney George Franklin Skipworth came into Eugene on the same train. He could not have been more surprised to see Bernard arrested. When Skipworth boarded the southbound train in Albany, about sixty miles north,

> *He sat down just in front of a young man who said, "How are you, Mr. Skipworth?" Mr. Skipworth responded to the salutation and then busied himself with a newspaper. The young man who addressed him was Claude Branson* [sic].[132]

Branton was arrested on the corner of Eighth and Oak Streets. Branton was surprised that he had been arrested and would not say a word about the incident. He was placed in the local jail, where he saw Courtland Green, and was taken aback at seeing him there. On his person, Branton carried "$40.31 in money, a new gold watch, and a pocket knife."[133]

Branton was arraigned quickly and entered a "not guilty" plea. He was held in jail until the preliminary examination on August 1, 1898.

John A. Linn, murdered by Claude Branton at Isham's Corral. 1898. *Lane County History Museum.*

Evidence began to compound against Branton. One Jess Holbrook, who was a mail carrier, said that Branton rode with him to Dexter, Oregon, from Big Prairie, Oregon. Branton tried to sell Holbrook his .38-caliber Smith & Wesson, with which he had killed Linn, for the sum of $3.00. He took the $2.75 that Holbrook offered instead and went on his way.[134] A.D. Hyland confirmed this, saying that Branton tried to sell him his horse and that he tried to sell the gun to Holbrook.[135]

The preliminary examination of Branton went as planned on August 1. All the people who had seen him after the murder were questioned, including those who were previously quoted here. Others came forward to say that Branton had tried to compel them to help him get rid of some horses or some saddles. Sheriff Withers testified about the diameter of the corral, the burned area and where the bones were found. Then he brought the box of bones forward for the jury. They deliberated but deferred judgment and sentencing until October.

On October 26, 1898, the grand jury formally charged Claude Branton with murder in the first degree in the case of John Linn.[136] His trial began on October 31. On November 1, Cortland Green jointly indicted with Branton for the murder, changed his plea to "guilty, and agreed to testify against Branton the following day. "The court decided to have Green come on the stand at 11 o'clock that morning, and shortly afterward Branton broke down and cried like a baby."[137]

During Green's testimony, on November 1, it was revealed that Branton shot Linn two times after he'd gone to sleep. He and Green put Linn's body on the coals and put wood on it so it burned through the night. The next day, they took the large bones out of the fire, smashed them with the flat section of the axe and put the remains back in the fire. They also burned the clothing and boot tops, though they threw away the rubber soles that wouldn't burn into the river. In the process, Linn's belongings, including the money he had in his pockets (seventy-five dollars) and the rest of his valuables, were stolen by Branton.[138] The testimony of the witnesses and Deputy Day and Sheriff Withers lasted a few days.

On the morning of November 4, 1898, shortly after eleven o'clock, the jury rendered a verdict of "guilty of murder in the first degree" in the case of Claude Branson. It was a premeditated act done for his own personal gain. It took the jury only forty-five minutes to make the decision.

Withers, Day and other guards were removing Branton back to the jail when suddenly, he jumped from Day's grasp and on to his person, trying to knock him down and take his gun from the holster. Branton was frenzied and was only wrested under control after Withers helped to subdue him. Branton yelled that if he could, he'd kill them both and Green too.[139]

The sentencing began on the morning of November 8. Judge Hamilton overruled the defense attorney's pleas for mistrial on the grounds of errors or mistaken jury instructions and sentenced Branton to death by hanging at 10:00 a.m. on December 22, 1898. Branton took the news quietly and without expression. His mother and sister wept openly in court as the verdict was read.

> *When asked if he had anything to say why sentence should not be passed upon him he replied in a clear and steady voice, "I have nothing to say."*[140]

Cortland Green was sentenced on November 10, 1898, to life imprisonment for his part in John Linn's death.

Branton did not take to his imprisonment well. The newspaper reported that he was causing concern within the jail itself and between other prisoners:

> *Claude Branton, the convicted murderer of John Linn, who is soon to be hanged, is as restless in the county jail as a caged lion. The other day he sent for Deputy District Attorney Harris, but had nothing particular to say, but several times tried to induce Mr. Harris to come within reaching distance of his cell. Monday evening he tried a number of times to have Sheriff Withers approach the cell closely, but was not accommodated. After the sheriff left he told the other prisoners that if Withers had come up to the cage he would have attempted to get his pistol, and would have*

> *used it with effect if he was successful. He also said that the officers were onto him, and that Harris had come within reaching distance he would have "choked him to death."*[141]

In Eugene, on December 17, preparations were underway for Branton's execution. Things had been rather slow because the court had been waiting to see if the Oregon Supreme Court would hand down a stay of execution. No motion had been put forth. On the morning of the seventeenth, then, the county ordered the materials they needed to get a thirty-five by forty-foot square that would be enclosed by a twelve-foot-tall fence. The department planned to cover the prisoner walkway to the scaffold with wire fencing as well. Hangings were still open for viewing at that time, and invitations went out to selected officials and individuals involved with the case.

A surprise stay of execution was given down by the Oregon Supreme Court. It was widely understood that the execution would then be delayed by at least six months.[142] Branton would not be hanged until the appeal was heard by the supreme court. On the day of his first scheduled execution date, the sheriff was inundated by as many as six hundred requests to witness Branton's death.

His legal team made requests and motions, and continuances were made to consider who exactly did what on the night Linn was killed. Then on March 3, 1899, Branton tried his most audacious attempt yet. During the switchover from the night watch to give the prisoner time to bathe and exercise, Branton tried to hold up the sheriff with a look-alike gun. The gun was actually carved from a raw potato covered in tinfoil. It was considered so ingenious that it was later put on display in the sheriff's office for anyone to come and see.[143]

The conversation around this breakout attempt was related in *The Plaindealer*, from Roseburg, Oregon:

> *All at once Branton exclaimed, "You are a Christian, ain't you, Mr. Withers?"*
>
> *Mr. Withers answered, "Yes."*
>
> *"If you were in here wouldn't you get out if it was possible?"*
>
> *The Sherriff good-naturedly said, "Yes," without looking up.*
>
> *Then Branton stepped back into the corridor where it was a little dark, and holding in his hand what resembled a navy six-shooter said loudly "Throw up your hands."*

> *Mr. Withers was amazed and thought Branton had by some means procured a gun, but kept his cool and said, "Oh, come off."*
>
> *In a few seconds Branton concluded that his ruse had been discovered and laughed, and claimed he meant "nothing." Later he stated that if it had been a real gun, he would have done some "real shooting."*[144]

In March, another appeal was mounted in Branton's defense. It was rejected, and the judge reaffirmed the guilty verdict. He officially faced his sentence of death by hanging charge for the murder of John Linn "on May 12, between the hours of 10 and 12 a.m."[145]

The scaffold and yard were readied after Branton had lost his final appeal. The public was allowed to walk up and inspect the gallows area for themselves, a gruesome tradition, and speculate on the prisoner's state of mind and ability to sleep through the construction. Petitions were advertised and circulated for "Friends of Claude Branton" to sign against the act of capital punishment, and local pastors made their pleas for mercy at the pulpit and in letters to the editors of various newspapers.

Invitations to the hanging were sent to sheriffs of other counties, individuals involved in the case and others who had shown interest. As before, many more requests for admittance were made than could be given.

Locals poked fun at Branton's impending fate in gossipy news columns. Their quips had a macabre, dark humor flare. "It is said Claude Branton the condemned murderer gets weak in the knees at times and begs for mercy," one wrote. "It is predicted by some that he will break down on the scaffold." Another commenter said with relish, "It is said that Claude Branton jumped two feet high when he heard that Governor Geer had pardoned Olberman (another prisoner). Today Claude will jump ten feet low because Geer did not pardon one Branton."[146] Sheriffs from other counties accepted the invitation and prepared to attend the "necktie party."

The *Gold Hill News* reported on Branton's frame of mind in the week or so before his death:

> *Claude Branton, the condemned murderer, has been playing "pedro (a card game)," the last few nights with Guard John Holland, and lost each night. In a jovial spirit he remarked to Holland after Sunday night's game that he would have to play a stiff game from now on to win the series.*[147]

Claude Branton went to bed at around eleven o'clock the evening before his execution. After writing some correspondence, he sealed them and

Execution of Claude Branton, 1899. Branton is the short, dark-haired man in the center of the scaffold facing the camera; Lane County Sheriff W.W. Withers holds the rope on the right. The man with his hand on Branton's shoulder is Henry Day. Two ministers are also on the platform. *Lane County History Museum.*

went to sleep. He went without breakfast but accepted clergy on the fateful morning to pray and sing with him from early until about 9:00 a.m. At 9:30 a.m., his family was allowed to visit and speak with the prisoner. After that, Sheriff Withers was obliged to read the warrant to Branton out loud.

At 10:45 a.m., Branton left his cell for the final time. He was calm and told everyone in the jail goodbye as he left. Sheriff Withers and other officers accompanied him for the walk to the scaffolding down the hall, down the steps and outside. He bequeathed a Bible to his mother, a white tie to his brother and the letters he had written the night before to be mailed after his death.

Branton was able to climb the scaffolding stairs to the trapdoor by himself. He was asked if he wanted to make a statement. "In a firm voice," the *Dalles Weekly Chronicle* reported, "he told those present that he did not want them to bear any ill-will against his people on his account." With a request for "sympathy and prayers," he "urged them to walk in God's way." All present agreed that Branton was calmer and more collected than any prisoner they had ever seen.

The trapdoor mechanism was pushed at 10:50 a.m. by Sheriff Withers. Branton fell through the trapdoor about five feet and within fifteen minutes was gone. The yard where the scaffold stood was packed in a crush of people. It was estimated that sixty people were in direct attendance, including those family members who wanted to be there, and that more than one thousand others were in the streets around the enclosure. It was reported that despite the large crowd, they were "quiet and orderly." After Branton was declared dead, he was cut down from the ropes and laid into a coffin for his family.[148]

In the aftermath of the execution, the Branton fervor that had overtaken the entire state of Oregon took a while to die down. Some of the final letters, travel sketches and poetry he wrote were published after his death. His last poem was printed in the *Bohemia Nugget*:

> *My confidence in Man*
> *Is as I have said;*
> *Three men can keep a secret*
> *Providing two of them are dead.*

Branton never confessed any remorse for the murder of John Linn, the theft of the horses or anything that he had done. He only looked for escape opportunity after opportunity, loophole on loophole. In the end, Claude Branton was only sorry that he hadn't had the chance to kill Cortland Green as well.[149]

12

"BETTER LOOKING THAN THE AVERAGE WOMAN"

E.S. Prindel and Justifiable Homicide

This story from the Lane County Coroner's Office in Eugene takes place a short drive to the west. Rose Case Johnson was at home late in the evening of Sunday, August 23, 1910, in the 160-acre farm she shared with her husband, John, or "Swede," Johnson. The couple's son, Benjamin, also called "Bennie," five, was playing inside while Rose stepped in the front garden of the home to answer the door.

In the coroner's inquest, Assistant District Attorney Skipworth found rumors about Rose Johnson that were, according to the social code of the time, elaborated on and published in his official report. It is an infuriating detail to today's mindset, he wrote that Rose "is a very pretty woman of the brunette type, did not bear the best reputation and her husband had suspected her for a long time of not being right."

He went on to say that Rose Johnson found John (Swede), her husband, to be "of a very jealous disposition," and that "she admitted that often she did things just to excite his jealousy." It seemed important for Skipworth to add that Rose Johnson was from Yaquina Bay and that she was "said to have a little Indian blood." The most interesting, and peculiar, line in the report stated that Rose was "better looking than the average woman found in the mountainous regions." Swede was suspicious of his wife, if later reports were to be believed. She was younger than his estimated thirty or thirty-two years of age and had been described as bright and energetic.

On the day of August 23, Swede Johnson had been on his job at a logging camp for some weeks, as was his habit. A neighbor, E.S. Prindel, who had long worked for a cheese factory nearby, had left his job on the afternoon of Saturday, the twenty-second, to visit a Miss Ada Weeks at her home. The two had been "keeping company" in Weeks's place on Fiddle Creek. On the way back to his job at the cheese factory, Prindel stopped to talk to Rose Johnson, as the Johnson farm was on the way between the two locations.[150]

Prindel was a friend of Swede Johnson but also was known to pester local women, including Rose. Later, the authorities would find out some of his past:

> *From a former resident who knew Prindel…it is learned that Prindle was the type of man that often gets into trouble of this kind. This man says that* [when they lived in] *Douglas County he was always trying to mix in family affairs, and was accused of being on intimate terms with a number of women.*[151]

The way Rose reported the story of that evening's events started:

> *Late Sunday evening, Prindel came along the road in front of the house afoot and stopped to talk with her. He asked if he might come into the house and she consented. The little boy, Bennie, soon became sleepy and was put to bed, after which Prindel made improper advances toward her.*[152]

Rose, horrified, tried to fight back and rebuff him, but she was considerably smaller, and Prindel succeeded in pulling her bodily up the stairs. "He succeeded in getting her half-way to a landing at the top of the stairway," she said.

Meanwhile, Swede Johnson and his suspicious mind could not rest. He set out from his logging camp early because he thought he might catch his wife in the act. He got to their house at about nine o'clock on August 23. In the dust approaching the home, he saw recent footsteps. They continued into his yard. Swede, who heard some voices inside, decided to sit under the side window to further investigate. He had just about convinced himself that someone was inside with his wife when he heard angry voices, possibly the commotion on the stairs, and went back to the front of the house.

The noise of the gate must have scared Prindel, because he ran out the back door. The darkness obscured his identity. Swede Johnson grabbed his gun, a 25-30 rifle, and shot "from the hip" as soon as he could reach the intruder. He didn't take the time to aim, as he meant to just frighten whoever was there.

The shot found its mark a little better than Swede had intended. He ran after the form, who had dropped, to see if he could help, and "was horrified to find that it was Prindel, whom he had considered one of his best friends."[153]

> *He soon returned and exclaimed, "Rose, I have killed my best friend." She then admitted to her husband, she says that he was there and he made improper advances, but she had repulsed them.*[154]

Swede tried to call some of the neighbors to tell them what had happened. After he could not reach anyone, he went to a house nearby, and two neighbors brought Prindel's body to the authorities. Swede Johnson went home to wait for the sheriff.

Matters were made extremely complicated by the fact that a huge multicounty fire had occurred to the northeast on August 23 that had burned down the town of Wendling and several logging camps in the area. The car holding Attorney Skipworth, Coroner Gordon, Deputy Sheriff Fisk and Sheriff Bown, the investigative team, was hampered by fires on the road en route from Eugene. It was so bad that they were surrounded by flames on three sides at times. "For half a mile, they were hemmed in by the fire and in danger of being trapped at any moment," reported the *Eugene Weekly Guard*.

Lumbering in Oregon in 1910. *From Joseph Gaston,* The Centennial History of Oregon, 1811–1911, *S.J. Clarke Publishing, 1912.*

> *The flames were so hot that they scorched their faces. On either side the fire was roaring and it was a most precarious position. The tall trees were crashing down on all sides of them and any moment they were in danger of being crushed by a falling tree.*[155]

A slightly amazing thing is the fact that the vehicle they were driving, most likely a Ford Model A or Model T with retractable top, was pushed to its top speed—forty miles per hour, paltry to the speed of cars today.

> *The road was good and Chauffeur Sweet opened the throttle until the light car was traveling at 40 miles an hour. The smoke was so thick that it was almost impossible to see ahead. It was with a feeling of relief that they soon reached the other side of the blaze.*

The Wendling Fire was one of the biggest and longest to burn in the area in 1910. It burned all but three of the homes in the logging camp and vicinity. The first fire was sparked by a lightning strike and was one of many to decimate areas of the country in 1910, a year known as "The Big Burn."[156]

The inquest, on August 24, was headed by that crew made up of Attorney Skipworth, Coroner Gordon, Deputy Sheriff Fisk and Sheriff Bown. A logger had even been hired to cut a fallen tree that was stuck in the middle of the road. They arrived as soon as possible and immediately interviewed all parties and inspected the site of the crime.

The jury was presented with this new evidence as well as the previous testimony. Rose Johnson showed that E.S. Prindel was the "superintendent of the Sunday School in that vicinity" and that "for a long time before Johnson arrived, talked of Sunday School affairs and a revival meeting that was being held there at the time."

She elaborated on the events that had taken place that Sunday and was able to state what had happened in a more precise way. She and Benny went to visit neighbors but otherwise had been alone that day. She had recently returned from the camp where Swede Johnson was logging. Rose was an occasional cook there. After visiting, she had made supper for herself and Benny and was sitting outside on the porch while he was playing when Prindel came up. It was near nine o'clock when this happened.

When he asked for water, she invited him inside and gave Benny his dinner, then "undressed him and put him to bed. Mr. Prindel was still there when I did that," she stated.

> *He stayed and we talked. He asked me when my husband was coming home.…He was telling me about the Sunday school and the revival meetings.…He said he was going away in a few days. After I had put my son to bed, we talked for a little while and I mentioned that it was getting late and he said that he thought so too.*[157]

Rose went on to describe the way Prindel tried to assault her and tried to pull her away:

> *Partly through force, he got me upstairs. I pleaded and begged with him. I don't know how long it was until the gate squeaked. He ran, and a moment later I heard a shot. Then my husband came in. He asked me who it was, and at first I was frightened. I said I didn't know. Then I said that it was Mr. Prindel. He said that he didn't know that Mr. Prindel was that kind of man, and that he only shot to scare him.*

On learning the intruder's identity, Swede Johnson was despondent.

> *He exclaimed, "Oh, my God, I have killed him!" He ran toward the house and grabbed the gun saying, "I've killed him and now I'm going to kill myself." I struggled with him and took the gun away.*

"One of the most damning pieces of evidence," said the prosecution, "was that Johnson was very angry with his wife and was in that same state of mind when he shot the man." The defense declared that Johnson, instead, was "disconsolate."[158]

They brought back a recommendation, which after going to the coroner's jury, was certified to send to the county. The verdict was "justifiable homicide."

The circuit court was to see the Prindel death as the first case when it convened on December 9, 1910.[159] Attorney Skipworth said,

> *The coroner's jury verdict of Justifiable Homicide was well received.… Everybody, even Prindel's brothers and other relatives, seemed satisfied with the decision.*[160]

Some of Rose and Swede Johnson's reports differ in whether he was suspected home on the evening of the tragedy. As well, one claim said that Rose wanted to leave with the sheriff and not come back after the shooting. This is unsubstantiated. Other accounts have the happy family driving off

Three men, one of them holding an axe; a woman; and four children standing at two doorways of a log cabin, circa 1903. *Library of Congress, Prints & Photographs Division.*

together in a car after the "not guilty" verdict. There is no personal statement from either party, or the coroner's office, to corroborate either end to the story. The people involved seemed to live in difficult, lonely circumstances in the best of cases, and hopefully things improved for Rose, Benny, and John "Swede" Johnson.

NOTES

1. The Murder of Sheriff W.W. Withers and the Last Hanging in Lane County

1. *Eugene Weekly Guard*, 1902.
2. *Eugene Weekly Guard*, 1902.
3. *Daily Capital Journal*, 1898.
4. *Corvallis Gazette*, 1901.
5. *Eugene Weekly Guard*, 1900.
6. *Junction City Bulletin*, 1901.
7. *Reward for arrest of Henry J. Day*, 1899.
8. *Eugene Weekly Guard*, 1903.
9. *Eugene Weekly Guard*, 1902.
10. *Eugene Weekly Guard*, 1902.
11. *The Leader*, 1903.
12. *Eugene Weekly Guard*, 1903.
13. *Eugene Weekly Guard*, 1903.
14. *Bohemia Nugget* 1903.
15. *Daily Journal*, 1903.
16. Cornelius and Huntington, *Eliott Lyons*, 2.
17. *Eugene Weekly Guard*, 1903
18. Death Penalty Information Center.
19. Carey, *Murder of Sheriff William*.
20. *Eugene Weekly Guard*, 1903.
21. *Eugene Weekly Guard*, 1906.

2. "More Than I Can Stand!": The Deaths of Sanford and Emma Skinner

22. *Eugene City Guard*, 1882.
23. *Morning Oregonian* 1905.
24. *Morning Oregonian*, 1905.
25. Day, *Skinner's Coroner Report*, 4.
26. Day, *Skinner's Coroner Report*, 5.
27. Day, *Skinner's Coroner Report*, 6.
28. *Cottage Grove Leader*, 1905.
29. Dawson, *All That Is Wicked*, 49
30. *Morning Oregonian*, 1905.
31. *The Plaindealer*, 1905.
32. *The Plaindealer*, 1905.
33. *Register-Guard*, 1948.
34. *Eugene Guard*, 1929.

3. "Come Help Me": Hermann and Lena Petersdorf

35. *Eugene Weekly Guard* 1900.
36. Smith, "Maria Rickli Schwader."
37. Smith, "Maria Rickli Schwader."
38. "Horse Powered Threshing," Old Oregon Photos.
39. Coldwell, "Beginnings of Electric Power," 25–36.
40. King, *Inquest into Deaths of Lina and Hermann.*
41. King, *Inquest into Deaths of Lina and Hermann.*
42. King, *Inquest into Deaths of Lina and Hermann.*
43. *Oregonian*, 1900.
44. King, *Inquest into Deaths of Lina and Hermann.*
45. *Oregonian*, 1900.
46. Smith, "Maria Rickli Schwader."
47. *Eugene Weekly Guard*, 1900.
48. "Our History," Mental Health America.
49. "How America's Mental Health System Evolved," CHAS.
50. Smith, interview.

4. Death by Donkey Engine: Misadventure in the Logging Camps and Mills of Eugene

51. McQuiddy, "Eugene."
52. *Eugene Weekly Guard*, 1902.

53. Miner, "State That Timber Built."
54. Kotar and Gessler, "Steam Donkey."
55. King, *Holt Testimony*.
56. Cheshire, *Holt Testimony*.
57. King, *Holt Testimony*.
58. Brown, *Holt Testimony*.
59. *Eugene Weekly Guard*, 1902.
60. *Eugene Weekly Guard*, 1902.
61. *Eugene Weekly Guard*, 1900.
62. Griffin, *Death of James P. Holce*.
63. DeMay, "Photos."
64. *Eugene Weekly Guard*, 1901.
65. Bieber, "10 Most Dangerous Jobs."

5. Illumination of Danger: Clifton Shriver

66. Kramer, "Eugene Water."
67. Kramer, "Eugene Water."
68. Mason *EWEB*, 3.
69. Brush, "Brush System."
70. Johnson, *Death of Clifton*.
71. *Eugene City Guard*, 1893.
72. *Eugene City Guard*, 1893.
73. Williams, *Death of Clifton*, 1893.
74. *Eugene City Guard*, 1893.

6. Theft and Law Enforcement: Henry J. Day

75. *Eugene City Guard*, 1889.
76. Mansky and Anderson, "Eight Secret Societies."
77. *Eugene City Guard*, 1894.
78. *Eugene City Guard*, 1899.
79. *Eugene City Guard*, 1899.
80. *Eugene Weekly Guard*, 1903.
81. Mike, "Henry Jackson Day."
82. Mike, letter.

7. The Long Pursuit of Bert Heaton

83. *The Plaindealer*, 1902.

84. *Democratic Times*, 1902.
85. *Sunday Oregonian*, 1902.
86. *Corvallis Times*, 1902.
87. *Oregon Daily Journal*, 1902.
88. *Corvallis Times*,1902.
89. Oglesby, *Physician*.

8. It's a Dangerous Business, Walking Out Your Door: Freak Accidents and Horrible Ways to Die

90. Williams, *Hattie Sumner Coroner's Report*.
91. Stromberg, "Real Story."
92. "Light Rail Vehicles," Encyclopedia.com.
93. *Michaels/Swartz/Bailey Coroner's Report*, 1908.
94. *Smith Coroner's Report*, 1908.
95. Schwartz, *Mount Coroner's Report*.
96. "Brickmaking in the USA," Brick Collecting.
97. Gordon, *Jessie Coroner's Report*.
98. Best, *William Powell's Coroner's Report*.
99. Best, *William Powell's Coroner's Report*.
100. Preston and Haines, *Fatal Years*, 1.
101. *Eugene Weekly Guard*, 1900.
102. *Eugene Weekly Guard*, 1908.
103. *Eugene Weekly Guard*, 1908.

9. The Siren Song of the Calliope: John Seymour

104. Elwell, "What 19th-Century Circus Life Was."
105. *Weekly Oregon Statesman*, 1903.
106. *Weekly Oregon Statesman*, 1903.
107. *Weekly Oregon Statesman*, 1903.
108. *Weekly Oregon Statesman*, 1903.
109. *Eugene Weekly Guard*, 1903.
110. *Morning Oregonian*, 1903.
111. *Albany Democrat*, 1904.
112. *Oregon Daily Journal*, 1904.
113. *The Oregonian*, 1904.

10. Prejudice Rampant: The Dark Violence of Inherent Racism in Eugene

114. Chambers, *Remarkable Oregon Women*, 56.
115. Chambers, *Remarkable Oregon Women*, 56.
116. Gregory, "Oregon Migration History."
117. Mealy, *Julia Fishman Coroner's Report*, 2.
118. Mealy, *Julia Fishman Coroner's Report*, 3.
119. Mealy, *Julia Fishman Coroner's Report*, 4.
120. Mealy, *Julia Fishman Coroner's Report*, 6.

11. Mayhem at Isham's Corral

121. *Athena Press*, 1898.
122. *Eugene City Guard*, 1898.
123. *Eugene City Guard*, 1898.
124. *Daily Capital Journal*, 1898.
125. *The Dalles Daily Chronicle*, 1898.
126. Powers, *J.A. Linn Coroner's Report*.
127. *Condon Globe*, 1898.
128. *Condon Globe*, 1898.
129. *The West*, 1898.
130. *The Dalles Daily Chronicle*, 1898.
131. *The Dalles Daily Chronicle*, 1898.
132. *Eugene City Guard*, 1898.
133. *Eugene City Guard*, 1898.
134. *Hillsboro Independent*, 1898.
135. *Eugene City Guard*, 1898.
136. *Daily Capital Journal*, 1898.
137. *The Dalles Daily Chronicle*, 1898.
138. *Valley Record*, 1898.
139. *Daily Capital Journal*, 1898.
140. *The Dalles Daily Chronicle*, 1898.
141. *Gold Hill News*, 1898.
142. *Condon Globe*, 1898.
143. *Heppner Gazette*, 1899.
144. *The Plaindealer*, 1899.
145. *Oregon Statesman*, 1899.
146. *Bohemia Nugget*, 1899.
147. *Gold Hill News*, 1899.
148. *The Dalles Weekly Chronicle*, 1899.
149. *Bohemia Nugget*, 1899.

12. "Better Looking Than the Average Woman": E.S. Prindel and Justifiable Homicide

150. *Oregon Daily Journal*, 1910.
151. *Eugene Weekly Guard*, 1910.
152. *Eugene Weekly Guard*, 1919.
153. *Oregon Daily Journal*, 1910.
154. *Eugene Weekly Guard*, 1919.
155. *Eugene Weekly Guard*, 1910.
156. LaLande, "Forest Fires."
157. *Twice-A-Week-Guard*, 1910.
158. *Twice-A-Week-Guard*, 1910.
159. *Twice-A-Week-Guard*, 1910.
160. *Eugene Weekly Guard*, 1919.

BIBLIOGRAPHY

Albany Democrat. "Bridal Trip with Burglar." May 20, 1904. https://oregonnews.uoregon.edu.

Athena Press. "Shot In The Head." July 8, 1898, https://oregonnews.uoregon.edu.

Best, William F. *William Powell's Coroner's Report*. Lane County Coroner, 1906.

Bieber, Christy, J.D. "10 Most Dangerous Jobs in America for 20245." Forbes. https://www.forbes.com.

Bohemia Nugget. "Eliott Lyons." March 13, 1903. https://oregonnews.uoregon.edu.

———. "News." May 12, 1899, 4. https://oregonnews.uoregon.edu/.

———. "News." May 19, 1899, 4. https://oregonnews.uoregon.edu.

Brick Collecting. "Brickmaking in the USA: A Brief History." https://brickcollecting.com.

Brown, Robert. *Holt Testimony*. Lane County Coroner, 1900.

Brush, Charles F. "The Brush System of Electric Lighting." *Scientific American*. April 2, 1881. https://www.scientificamerican.com.

Carey, Russ. "The Murder of Sheriff William Washington Withers." Unpublished manuscript, 2016.

Chambers, Jennifer. *Remarkable Oregon Women: Revolutionaries & Visionaries*. The History Press, 2015.

The CHAS Foundation. "How America's Mental Health System Evolved." https://thechasfoundation.org.

Cheshire, N.L. *Holt Testimony*. Lane County Coroner, 1900.

Coldwell, O.B. "Beginnings of Electric Power in Oregon." *Oregon Historical Quarterly* 31, no. 1 (1930): 25–36.

Condon Globe. "John Linn Murdered." July 14, 1898, 3. https://oregonnews.uoregon.edu.

———. "Local News." December 22, 1898, 3. https://oregonnews.uoregon.edu.
Cornelius, Ray, and Hallie H. Huntington. 1976. *Eliott Lyons & Sheriff Withers*. Eugene, OR: n.p. Transcription of audio cassette tape.
Corvallis Gazette. August 13, 1901. https://oregonnews.uoregon.edu.
Corvallis Times. "Benton Tracy." November 15, 1902. https://oregonnews.uoregon.edu.
Cottage Grove Leader. "Murder." June 3, 1905, 1. https://oregonnews.uoregon.edu.
CPI Inflation Calculator. "Inflation from 1899 to 2024." https://www.in2013dollars.com.
Daily Capital Journal. "Arrested." July 12, 1898, 4. https://oregonnews.uoregon.edu.
———. "Claude Branton Indicted." October 28, 1898, 4. https://oregonnews.uoregon.edu.
———. December 20, 1898. https://oregonnews.uoregon.edu.
———. "Two Oregon Murderers." November 4, 1898, 1. https://oregonnews.uoregon.edu.
Daily Journal. "Eliott Lyons Convicted." March 5, 1903. https://oregonnews.uoregon.edu.
The Dalles Daily Chronicle. "Execution of Branton." November 10, 1898, 1. https://oregonnews.uoregon.edu.
———. "Execution of Claude Barton." May 17, 1899, 1. https://oregonnews.uoregon.edu.
———. "Pled Guilty to Murder." November 2, 1898, 2. https://oregonnews.uoregon.edu.
———. "Wanted at Eugene." July 9, 1898, 3. https://oregonnews.uoregon.edu.
———. "Wayside Gleanings." July 16, 1898, 3. https://oregonnews.uoregon.edu.
———. "Wayside Gleanings." July 22, 1898, 3. https://oregonnews.uoregon.edu.
Dawson, Kate W. *All That Is Wicked: A Gilded-Age Story of Murder and the Race to Decode the Criminal Mind*. Penguin Publishing Group, 2022.
Day, F.M. *Skinner's Coroner Report*. Lane County Coroner, 1905.
Death Penalty Information Center. "Oregon." https://deathpenaltyinfo.org.
DeMay, Daniel. 2019. "Photos: A Tale of the Northwest's Logging Past." Seattle PI. https://www.seattlepi.com.
Democratic Times. "A Murderer Arrested." July 23, 1902, 3. https://oregonnews.uoregon.edu.
Elwell, Mina. "What 19th-Century Circus Life Was Really Like." Grunge. https://www.grunge.com.
Encyclopedia. "Light Rail Vehicles." https://www.encyclopedia.com.
Eugene City Guard. "Accident." June 10, 1882. https://www.findagrave.com.
———. "Captured." July 23, 1898, 7. https://oregonnews.uoregon.edu.
———. "Death by Electrocution." January 7, 1893. https://oregonnews.uoregon.edu.
———. "Developments Made to Date." July 9, 1898, 4. https://oregonnews.uoregon.edu.

———. "Henry J. Day." November 4, 1899, 6. https://oregonnews.uoregon.edu.
———. "Items." May 26, 1894. https://oregonnews.uoregon.edu.
———. "Right and Honorable." November 4, 1899. https://oregonnews.uoregon.edu.
———. "A Sad Betrayal of Trust." November 4, 1899, 2. https://oregonnews.uoregon.edu.
———. "Unity Items." July 30, 1898, 4. https://oregonnews.uoregon.edu.
Eugene Guard. "Lloyd W. Skinner." June 27, 1929. https://www.findagrave.com.
Eugene Weekly Guard. "An Accident." November 9, 1901. https://oregonnews.uoregon.edu.
———. "Brevities." October 25, 1902.
———. "Brutal Wife Murder." September 22, 1900.
———. "A Busy Man." February 1, 1902.
———. "Circus Notes." September 5, 1903.
———. "Coroner's Jury Verdict Is Approved." August 25, 1910, 1.
———. "Died." February 20, 1908, 5.
———. "Drove Automobile 40 MPH." August 25, 1910, 1
———. "Drowned." August 23, 1902.
———. "E.E. Lyons Hanged." April 18, 1903.
———. "Fatal Accident." March 1, 1902.
———. February 21, 1903.
———. "Henry J. Day Seen South." May 2, 1903.
———. "Killed by a Falling Tree." September 6, 1902, 1.
———. "Lyons Caught." February 14, 1903.
———. May 19, 1900.
———. "Murderer Interviewed." February 14, 1903.
———. "News from the County Clerk's Office." November 1, 1906.
———. October 20, 1900.
———. "A Peculiar Fatality." November 10, 1900, 7.
———. "Probate Court." October 6, 1900.
———. "W.W. Withers." April 19, 1902.
Find a Grave. "Lena S. *Skinner* Veach." https://www.findagrave.com.
Gold Hill News. "State News Notes." December 10, 1898, 1. https://oregonnews.uoregon.edu.
———. "State News Notes." May 13, 1899, 1.
Gordon, W.T. *Jessie Coroner's Report*. Lane County Coroner, 1909.
Gregory, James. 2018. "Oregon Migration History 1850-2018." America's Great Migration Project. https://depts.washington.edu.
Griffin, G.W. *Death of James P. Holce*. Lane County Coroner, 1900.
Heppner Gazette. "Branton Tries a Ruse." March 2, 1899, 3. https://oregonnews.uoregon.edu.

Hillsboro Independent. "Sufficiently Striking." July 29, 1898, 1. https://oregonnews.uoregon.edu.

Johnson, Lottie. *Death of Clifton Stevens*. Lane County Coroner, 1893.

Junction City Bulletin. March 21, 1901. https://oregonnews.uoregon.edu.

King, Archie. *Holt Testimony*. Lane County Coroner, 1900.

King, Dr. C. *Inquest into Deaths of Lina and Hermann Petersdorf*. Eugene, OR, 1900.

Kotar, S.L., and J.E. Gessler. "Steam Donkey." Wikipedia. https://en.wikipedia.org.

Kramer, George. "Eugene Water & Electric Board (EWEB)." Oregon Encyclopedia. https://www.oregonencyclopedia.org.

LaLande, Jeff. "Forest Fires of 1910." Oregon Encyclopedia. https://www.oregonencyclopedia.org.

Lane County History Museum. "Reward for the Arrest of Henry J. Day." https://lchm.pastperfectonline.com.

The Leader. "Lyons Is Taken." February 13, 1903. https://oregonnews.uoregon.edu.

Mansky, Jackie, and Sonja Anderson. "Eight Secret Societies You Probably Haven't Heard Of." *Smithsonian Magazine*, March 20, 2024. https://www.smithsonianmag.com.

Mason, George C. *EWEB: The First 100 Years*. Oregon Historical Society, 2011. https://www.eweb.org.

McQuiddy, Steve. "Eugene." Oregon Encyclopedia. https://www.oregonencyclopedia.org.

Mealy, J.S. *Julia Fishman Coroner's Report*. Lane County Coroner, 1891.

Mental Health America. "Our History." https://www.mhanational.org.

Michaels/Swartz/Bailey Coroner's Report. Lane County Coroner, 1908.

Mike, Jan A. "Henry Jackson Day." Find a Grave. https://www.findagrave.com.

———. "Sanford and Emma Skinner." Find a Grave. https://www.findagrave.com.

Miner, Tara Rae. "The State That Timber Built." *Oregon Humanities*, April 8, 2012. https://oregonhumanities.org.

Morning Oregonian. "Family Quarrel Costs Two Lives." June 2, 1905. https://oregonnews.uoregon.edu.

———. "Seymour Again in Jail." September 4, 1903, 14.

Oglesby, William W. *Physician*. Lane County Coroner, 1901.

Old Oregon Photos. "Horse Powered Threshing near Cottage Grove - c. 1903." https://www.oldoregonphotos.com.

Oregon Daily Journal. "J. Johnson Not Guilty." December 10, 1910, 3. https://oregonnews.uoregon.edu.

———. "Suburban News." July 30, 1902, 3.

———. "Takes Burglar on Wedding Tour." May 17, 1904, 12.

Oregonian. "Man Without Conscience." May 18, 1904, 12. https://oregonnews.uoregon.edu.

———. "Murdered His Wife." September 19, 1900, 4.

Oregon Statesman. "Will Soon Hang." April 7, 1899, 1. https://oregonnews.uoregon.edu.

The Plaindealer. "Branton Again." March 2, 1899, 3. https://oregonnews.uoregon.edu.

———. "Lane County Murderer." June 29, 1905, 1.

———. "Lane County Murderer Caught." July 21, 1902, 1.

Powers, A.S. *J.A. Linn Coroner's Report*. Lane County Coroners, 1898.

Preston, Samuel H., and Michael R. Haines. *Fatal Years*. Princeton University Press, 1991.

Robbins, William G. "Timber Industry." Oregon Encyclopedia. https://www.oregonencyclopedia.org.

Schwartz, J.C. *Mount Coroner's Report*. Lane County Coroner, 1898.

Smith, J. "Hermann August Edward Petersdorf, (25 Dec 1863–17 Sep 1900)." Find a Grave. https://www.findagrave.com.

———. "Lina Fluckiger Petersdorf (19 May 1869–17 September 1900)." Find a Grave. https://www.findagrave.com.

Smith, Joel. *Interview of J. Smith*. Salem, OR, 2024.

———. "Maria Rickli Schwader." Find a Grave. https://www.findagrave.com.

Smith Coroner's Report. Lane County Coroner, 1908.

Stromberg, Joseph. "The Real Story Behind the Demise of America's Once-Mighty Streetcars." *Vox*, May 7, 2015. https://www.vox.com.

Sunday Oregonian. "Back with Alleged Murderer." July 27, 1902, 6. https://oregonnews.uoregon.edu.

Twice-A-Week-Guard. "County Items." December 8, 1910, 5. https://oregonnews.uoregon.edu.

———. "John S. Johnson Set Free." December 12, 1910, 8.

Valley Record. "Trial of John Linn's Murderers." November 3, 1898, 3. https://oregonnews.uoregon.edu.

Webster, Ian. CPI Inflation Calculator. http://www.cpiinflationcalculator.com.

Weekly Oregon Statesman. "A Splendid Exhibition." August 28, 1903, 5. https://oregonnews.uoregon.edu.

———. "Was Tired of Prison Life." August 28, 1903, 5.

The West. "A Terrible Crime." July 15, 1898, 3. https://oregonnews.uoregon.edu.

Williams, Charles. *Death of Clifton Stevens*. Lane County Coroner, 1893.

Williams, S.R. *Hattie Sumner Coroner's Report*. Lane County Coroner, 1908.

Wilson, Bob. "Skinner Headstone." Find a Grave. https://www.findagrave.com.

ABOUT THE AUTHOR

Jennifer Chambers is a writer, publisher and host of *Chronic & Iconic* and *Same Crime, Different Time* podcasts. A former columnist and co-owner of a publishing company, she founded the TEDxVenetaWomen event and has spoken at conferences across the United States. After surviving a traumatic brain injury that erased her memory before age fifteen, she relearned everything from walking to speaking. She writes fantasy and paranormal books in addition to nonfiction.

For more information, see www.jennifer-chambers.com
or Instagram at @jennifer_chambers_